A Clay Pot Named Hazel

By Leigh Parcel

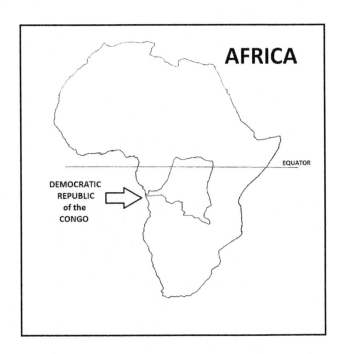

AFRICA

EQUATOR

DEMOCRATIC
REPUBLIC
of the
CONGO

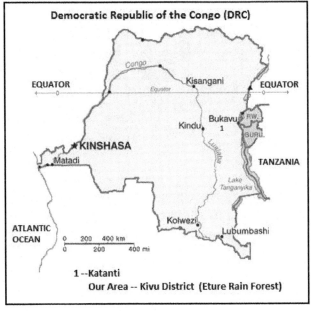

Democratic Republic of the Congo (DRC)

Congo

EQUATOR   Kisangani   EQUATOR
              Equator

                                    Bukavu RW.
                          Kindu   1
                                              BURU.
★KINSHASA
   Matadi   TANZANIA

                                    Lake
                                  Tanganyika

ATLANTIC   Kolwezi
OCEAN   0   200   400 km   Lubumbashi
           0   200   400 mi

       1 --Katanti
         Our Area -- Kivu District (Eture Rain Forest)

An Oklahoma girl, whose life spans more than 100 years, became a missionary nurse and served in Congo twenty years where she raised and taught five children.

TREE ON FRONT COVER

The tree is of an actual acacia tree which stood on our Katanti Station. It was a forest tree which had been left when the site was cleared for the station. I passed it every day and enjoyed its structure. I wanted its beauty saved for others to enjoy, so I made a sketch of it. That was fifty years ago; it is still a treasured reminder of my life in the rainforest of central Africa.

The clay pot is there to remind us that we are all humble humans, moldable as clay. God, the Master Potter, can shape us into articles of usefulness and beauty if we yield to His skillful hands.

DEDICATION

I dedicate this book to my four daughters: Joy, Merry Sue, Gay and Melodie, my son "Happy" (Leonard Leigh), and my husband Leonard. Joy and Happy were five and four when we arrived in Congo, 1945, and Melodie was six when we left, 1964. At various times each child had an important part in our missionary experiences. My dear husband was the only one to go with me all the way.

My gratitude goes to all the friends and relatives who urged me to write this book. Because of their encouragement and prayers, it has grown into a record of our African adventures as well as my life before and after. Many friends helped along the way. Some corrected manuscripts; others helped with organization, art work, and computer problems. My special thanks go to my daughter Joy, my editor, and my computer guru. To all these I give much gratitude and thank the Lord for each of them.

FOREWORD

One day I was visiting with a friend and happened to recount an incident of my life in Congo. She found it very interesting and commented that I really should write a book about my various adventures. I replied that I didn't think many people would be interested and that my life had been quite ordinary. She insisted that it would be very entertaining and informative. So I began to think about it. Several other friends and relatives also suggested that I write about my experiences in Congo. So I finally decided to try. I sat down before my computer, determined to learn how to use it.

The book started to be only about Congo and our journeys there and back, but my daughters were not satisfied. They wanted a record of all of my life and not just that segment. True, I had spent twenty important years in Africa, but I had also spent about thirty years before and fifty years after in other places. So now it has become an autobiography covering 101 years.

It was daughter Joy who suggested as a name for the book, *A Clay Pot Named Hazel*. Many, many years ago clay pots were very common and ordinary. Every family had several. They were much appreciated for their usefulness, if not for beauty.

My full name is Hazel Leigh. Through childhood and youth, I was known by the double name. Later, it seemed that people did not like to be bothered by two names, so they started calling me Hazel. I decided that if I was to have only one name, I would choose Leigh. In thinking of a name for the book, it seemed more appropriate to use Hazel. As the book begins with an ordinary childhood, so this name seems more humble and ordinary. Leigh is the name of my English ancestors, the family of Leigh of Warwickshire, England.

The Bible tells about the potter. He takes clay and skillfully shapes it with his potter's wheel and his hands into any shape he desires. My life began in a very ordinary way, but the Master Potter took my lump of clay and worked with it. I admit I was not always pliable to His hands, but He never gave up. I certainly was not perfect; I made many mistakes, but now I look back and rejoice in the ways He has molded my life. He has always protected, provided and guided. He has given me a worthwhile life.

It is true I really have been able to see and do many interesting things. In my youth I pledged to go to Africa to work alongside the indigenous people. Through that I have been given many privileges. I thank God for guiding and protecting me these many years. I gave him a little and He has rewarded me greatly. The best is yet to come: a glorious, eternal home in Heaven. As it is said, "You can't outgive God."

TABLE OF CONTENTS

CHAPTER ONE

MY EARLY LIFE

Early on a winter morning in 1912 in Tulsa, Oklahoma, the telephone in my paternal grandmother's house rang sharply. It was my father calling to tell his mother that she had just become a grandmother. The doctor had just left (remarkably, a female doctor delivered me) and mother and daughter were doing fine. He wanted his mother to come right away to see her first grandchild, me! But this was Sunday morning and she was scheduled to teach a Bible class. She promised to come just as soon as possible. After church she walked over a mile to my maternal grandparents' house to see and hold the tiny new baby.

There was a heated discussion as to my name. My mother wanted to name me Hazel after her sister, but Grandmother preferred Elvira after her mother. Elvira Leigh was part of my family heritage from an aristocratic English family, the Leighs of Warwickshire. Grandmother was quite proud of having such a famous heritage. Finally, they compromised on the name Hazel Leigh. I had no objections and everybody was happy. I was known as this double name for many years, but people seemed to prefer shorter names, so I chose, simply, Leigh.

My mother and father loved me very much and were very proud of their first child. After a week or so we went to one of my grandfather's farms in central Oklahoma. My father had lived on farms most of his life and knew how to farm with horse power. I had a normal infancy, developed well and learned to walk at ten months, they say. We were a very happy little family. But when I reached one year, tragedy struck. My father was injured in a farm accident and died. My mother was left alone with a child to support. Back in Tulsa, she worked in a department store awhile. Then she met a rancher from Colorado and married him. So we moved to western Colorado.

I had a carefree childhood on the ranch. I loved playing in the barnyard, the apple orchard and irrigation ditch. I was fascinated by our man-made cave. It was wide enough for a farm wagon to drive all the way through. Shelves on the sides were used to store potatoes, onions and apples. It had a delightful farm aroma that I still remember. We had a fine vegetable and berry garden, and lovely flowers: iris, gladiolas, peonies, and little yellow roses. My mother's sister, husband and two daughters lived on the same place. The girls were just a little older than I, and we had great times together, building model villages of maple syrup cans, enjoying picnics in the orchard, rolling down haystacks, watching cattle and horses, and petting dogs and kittens. I was scared of the big rooster, though.

There was an irrigation ditch between our house and the apple orchard. I loved to watch the water flowing along in the ditch and tried floating objects downstream. If I were on the other side, I could easily jump across the ditch. Once though, I tried this and, lo and behold, someone had put up a fence right before the ditch. I hopped across and into that barbed-wire fence. It made a long scratch, just missing my right eye. My mother cared for that most carefully, guarding my eye and hoping there would not be an ugly scar on my face.

All was going fine until it was time to go to school. The school bus was a covered wagon. In cold windy weather, students had to wait for the wagon in unsheltered places. School was simple and old-fashioned. My paternal grandmother back in Tulsa didn't think that would do for her oldest grandchild. She lived five short blocks from a good, up-to-date school. The weather was warmer and I could easily walk to school, so Grandmother offered me a home with her and Grandpa.

I'm sure it was hard for my mother to let me go, but she thought it would be best for me. By that time she had two smaller daughters, my half-sisters. I can't remember being distressed at leaving my mother. It was what was expected of me and I would just do it. I was glad to be going to school. I was nearly seven and fall semester would soon start. The problem was how to get back to Tulsa.

A woman who was coming east from California would be willing to chaperone me for the train trip. My grandmother came to Pueblo to meet me. Grandmother was kind to me, but I soon found out that she could be stern and I had better mind her. First, we had breakfast in the hotel and then she took me to a shoe store and bought a decent pair of shoes for me. We boarded the train, arriving home in early evening. I vividly remember the trip from the station in the big city, up the lighted avenue to home. And so, I moved back to Tulsa.

TULSA SCHOOL YEARS

I soon got acquainted with my new home. Grandmother's house was a very modest frame house of one and one-half stories. The attic had been nicely finished and served as added room when needed.

Beside this room was a lovely screened-in sleeping porch. This was especially appreciated in hot weather. Downstairs were living and dining rooms, two bedrooms, kitchen and bath. We had running water for hands, baths and laundry, and a well with a pump handle beside the back door for cooking and drinking water. For cooking, heating and lights we had gas. It was only a bit nicer than our ranch home.

I was about nine before we acquired modern appliances. I remember our first electric iron, fan, and vacuum cleaner which were great achievements! We also bought a Maytag washing machine which ran on kerosene. A telephone was needed for Grandpa's business; it was the kind that had a receiver on a long cord hanging on a hook beside the speaker. Our telephone number was "Osage, two one, two one" and calls went through a central switchboard with an operator who said, "Number, please." At that time Grandpa was superintendent of Tulsa city streets and was always busy.

We had a Ford roadster with only a front seat for business and another car with front and back seats for the family. The automobile industry was off to a good start and airplanes were just being tried out. Our street and sidewalks were not paved. There was a nice lawn in front and a larger yard in back with clotheslines, garden space, several fruit trees, a walnut tree, a chicken coop and a two-car garage which had been a horse barn when my grandparents first came to Tulsa. Grandma had some lovely flowers: iris, sweet peas, roses and a wisteria vine over the back porch.

I enjoyed school and attended that elementary school from first to seventh grade. Then the idea of junior high was started. The Tulsa educational system was very good and up-to-the-minute on modern trends. I had the advantage of a very good education. When I was in the fifth-grade geography class, I learned about Sao Paulo, Brazil, one of the fastest-growing and largest cities in the world. I never dreamed that I would have a daughter who would marry a Brazilian and live in Sao Paulo.

I also enjoyed playing with the neighbor children. We liked activities such as jump rope, hopscotch, hide and seek, and roller skating. I had two special friends my age next door; however, we could not go to school together because they went to the nearby Catholic school. Beside school and homework, Grandmother taught me the usual housekeeping tasks and sewing, knitting and crocheting. I have always liked to sew. Also, I took piano lessons. At first I used an old-fashioned pump organ, but one day when I was at school, my grandmother traded in the organ for a piano. I became a Girl Scout and had lots of fun times and learned many useful things. It was good for me to have the association with other girls since I had had no siblings at home.

Soon I started junior high where I took Latin and algebra. I also enjoyed swimming and art classes. I felt quite sophisticated. Life was going on quite pleasantly until tragedy struck, again! My grandfather was killed in a farm accident. He owned several farms in the area and was checking on the renters of one when the accident occurred. There was an explosion with some equipment using kerosene. Grandpa was badly burned and died soon after. All was changed for Grandma and me.

We received a small income from the farms and oil wells, but soon Grandmother realized she must find some way to earn a living. The best she could arrange was to operate a rooming house. She found a large, once elegant, house near downtown, right on Main Street. I was devastated to leave our home and friends, but it was necessary. Though I never did enjoy living there, one good thing was that it was near the high school and our Methodist church, so I could walk to town, school, church, and everywhere.

The spring after Grandpa's death and before we moved, I had a wonderful experience. My mother came from Western Colorado to see me and her mother and sister. She brought her youngest child, my little brother, whom I had never seen. I had not seen my mother for about eight years, all the time I had lived in Tulsa. You can imagine what a happy time we had together! I learned later that she had come expecting to take me back with her, but because Grandma was now a widow, she felt she should not take me away from her. I did not know this, but still I felt extremely sad when she and little brother Lucius left.

And so we moved to a big old house on Main Street. It had a wrap-around veranda, both ends of which had been closed in to make rentable sleeping rooms. It had three floors and could house five families and three or four single people. With all this, we had only one bathroom and one telephone! How did we ever manage? It took a lot of work to maintain everything. I could help Grandma some with cleaning and dishwashing, though I was quite busy with school. I had started high school soon after our move.

In high school I majored in science and math. Trigonometry I enjoyed but was nearly swamped by advanced algebra. Beside the required subjects, I took sewing, typing and art, and for physical education I took swimming and lifesaving classes. In one math class I was the only girl. I worked very hard for I didn't want those fellows to say that girls were too dumb to understand math. I wasn't at the top of the class, but did quite well.

In due time, I graduated in a class of over 600. I was in the Junior Honor Society and rated in the top eight percent of my class. But what was ahead for me? It was deep in the Depression; jobs and money were scarce. I did find a little work, but mostly sewed for customers on a private basis to earn a little money. Almost every day we had navy beans to eat.

Grandmother had taken me to her church ever since I had moved to Tulsa. I learned many Bible stories and memorized verses, but I knew little about Jesus and that He had died to provide my salvation. I was at Sunday School one morning, waiting for class to begin, when a messenger from the primary department appeared. He said that one of their teachers could not come. Would some teen like to substitute for her class? I really was not paying much attention, but somehow I got the message. I thought that I was not the type to do such a spur-of-the-moment thing; I had never wanted to be a teacher. I didn't know much about little children and didn't even know what the lesson was about and was not prepared. But I felt a strong urging that this was for me! So reluctantly and a bit scared, I went down to the primary group. Someone handed me a lesson book and sat me down at a table of first graders. I found this not so bad; in fact, I enjoyed it. One session and I was hooked. I never did go back to my usual Sunday School class.

Although I did not realize it at the time, now, looking back, I realize that day was the crucial point of my young life. It was as though God lifted me up, turned me around and set me down in the way I should go. Ever after, He has guided me step by step into a happy, worthwhile life. I am glad I made that first, reluctant step of obedience.

The superintendent of the children's department took me under her wing and helped me adjust to this work. She took me to Sunday School conventions, teaching seminars, and Bible classes. We had to walk to most of these places or ride a streetcar or bus. One Bible class was taught by Mrs. Colgan from Philadelphia School of the Bible. I had not had such comprehensive teaching before and enjoyed it very much. From that time, I really wanted to learn what the Bible was all about. I knew many stories and lessons, but how did they fit together? What was the real message? What was its purpose?

About this time we got a new pastor for our church. Other pastors had told us to be good, be kind to our neighbors, and give money to the church. This new pastor told us that we were all sinners and in need of a savior. He told us who Jesus was and about His death on the cross to atone for our sins. He said that each one of us must make a decision to accept Him and the salvation He provided, in order to be saved. I made that decision when I was about seventeen. Great joy filled my heart and I felt great relief that my sins were forgiven. I well remember that Sunday evening! As I left the church, I could not feel the floor under my feet; truly, I was walking on air. Jesus, the Heavenly Father, and the Holy Spirit have ever since been my helpers, protectors, providers, guides and companions.

Then, more than ever, I enjoyed the Bible studies taught by Mrs. Colgan. Her husband also taught Bible classes. One summer they took a trip west and visited Denver. There they found a wonderful Bible school where poor students could work for room, board and tuition. I had a deep desire for more schooling, but there was no money for college. Here was an opportunity, not only for education but also to learn Bible truths at Denver Bible Institute. My grandmother was getting to be an old woman and not strong enough for heavy housework. I'm sure she hated to see me go, but she felt it was the Lord's provision for me and he would care for her, also.

This was still during the Depression. A man had put an ad in the paper saying that he was driving to Colorado and would be glad to take passengers to help pay for his trip. Another Tulsa girl was ready to go to Denver Bible Institute too, and so we went to Denver with this strange man. We were two days on the trip and arrived safely at the campus on West Colfax Avenue.

BIBLE SCHOOL

Denver Bible Institute (DBI) was a small four-year college-level Bible school. It was on a small campus in a western suburb of Denver with two main buildings and a barn. Several old houses were rented to provide more dorm space. There were about seventy students, most of whom were as poor as I and we all worked for the school. Students did all the usual housekeeping tasks and some rather unusual jobs, such as working in the print shop, caring for livestock (cows, goats, turkeys and chickens) and raising garden vegetables. As I had done lots of sewing, I was put in the sewing department. We sewed, repaired and altered clothes for staff members. When other work was necessary, the sewing group was called to help out. The staff members worked for very small salaries but food, housing, laundry and sewing were provided.

I did mostly sewing, but before the course was finished, I had done all manner of jobs, including picking produce from the garden, cleaning crystal chandeliers, and sewing seat covers for cars. Some students went home for the summers, but I could not afford the trips or loss of credit for the next year. I stayed right there for four and one-half years. One summer the school was given a quantity of vegetables, more than could be used right then, so we did a lot of canning. It was done at night as the big cook stove was needed for meals during the day.

Leonard was also on the canning crew. At one point, we two, alone, were assigned to work with a spare stove in another location. I often laugh and say that Leonard and I spent several nights together before we were married, or even engaged.

The studies were intense. We studied the Bible by verses, chapters, books and subjects. We did lots of memory work and took tough exams every two months. There were a few other courses available, such as English grammar, public speaking, Greek, Spanish or French, homiletics, and several music classes. Most classes were lectures and we took our own notes.

In addition to daily classes, we were each assigned to some sort of Christian service on Sundays. Three teams, a fellow and a girl, were assigned to hold Sunday School and church services at small rural churches in an area north of Denver, close to Boulder. The fellows were the pastors and preachers, and the ladies, teachers and pianists. I was assigned to work with a classmate, a young man from Nebraska, Leonard Parcel. Since this was quite a long trip, we had opportunity to visit and get acquainted even though there were strict rules about the mingling of the sexes. This was our work for one year and then new assignments were made. Leonard and I were surprised that we had the same assignment as the previous year. (Did someone have ideas?)

To help us learn to work with different types of people, students changed roommates every two months. Moving days were "fruit basket upset" as we moved and settled in different rooms with different girls. As Christian workers, we needed to learn to love people who had different personalities, different tastes and habits. Many of the rooms were double rooms in the nice dorm; others were in dorm conditions, and still others in various houses in the neighborhood that the school had been able to rent.

In spite of the strict rules, we students, both fellows and ladies, did have great times together. We had a great picnic in the mountains each fall and spring, school parties once in awhile, and sometimes smaller group parties. My best friend, Hilda, lived at the school, but she had a home in Denver and we were invited there several times.

During our junior year, a missionary who had served a term in Africa visited. She persuaded the school to found a new mission to work in an unreached area in the rainforest of Congo. This would be a pioneer work. Many students were interested and applied to this mission; among them were Leonard and I, individually. We were accepted and began to make plans for this venture. I felt that I could be of more use if I knew more about medical situations; I decided to take nurse's training, but how?

The summer after graduating from DBI in 1936, I went to Oregon to visit my mother whom I had not seen for about six years. Also, I had sisters that I had never met. When the summer ended, Mother asked about my next move. Learning that I wanted to become a nurse, she suggested I go to San Bernardino, California, where relatives of my stepfather lived. A good school of nursing was located there and they offered to pay my bus fare. So I moved to San Bernardino.

JUNIOR COLLEGE AND PRE-NURSING

The first year of training was at the local junior college. There I studied basic sciences: anatomy, physiology, bacteriology, and chemistry. I did all right although I was three weeks late in starting. For anatomy class we dissected cats preserved in formaldehyde. Each group had a special cat; we called ours Pickle Puss. Another group named their cat Butch. We also worked on live frogs, but ours jumped out the upstairs window. We brought him back upstairs and finished our experiments with the poor thing.

The "almost relatives" were very helpful, as well as being good friends. One of my sisters and a niece were living with them. Both were named Mary, so my sister whose full name was Mary Evelyn became Marilyn. I found a domestic job which paid my room and board, and I could take the streetcar to the college. We all went to a good church. I made it through the first year quite well. Leonard wrote me a few times and I answered; it was just in friendship, or so I thought.

Before long the second year would begin. I returned to Colorado because I was given a scholarship to a Methodist school in Colorado Springs. Grandma was then living in a Denver suburb with my uncle and family. I had just a few days to visit them before time for school.

I must have written Leonard that I was coming back east. He came to see me and suggested that we go to a meeting; we had an enjoyable evening together. That was indeed a memorable evening, for it was then that Leonard proposed that we two should go to Congo together as man and wife. I was thrilled, of course, but a little bewildered; I put him off.

COLORADO SPRINGS

The next day my uncle took me to the hospital in Colorado Springs to begin the hospital phase of my training. I was excited to actually be working and studying in a hospital. I was thrilled to think that Leonard loved me, but I was completely up in the air. I got off to a good start at the hospital and began intensive classes as well as simple nursing tasks. As soon as I had a weekend off, I made a quick run to Denver. Leonard met me and we went for a walk near the DBI building (an unheard-of event during school days) and I told him that I would like very much to be his wife. We shared our first kiss right there on the sidewalk. Truly, it was thrilling to be in love and engaged. Later that evening, Leonard took me to the bus station for my return trip. We lingered as long as we dared, bidding a fond farewell. Finally, the bus driver said, "Well, kiss him again and then we'd better be off." Was I embarrassed!

I returned to routine but with a new song in my heart. I studied and worked hard, for I knew I must know these things when I got to Africa. Leonard was traveling for the mission, trying to gain financial and prayer support. When he could, he came to visit me. Once when he came, I was working night duty. I was so happy to see him I stayed up all day to be with him. I was terribly sleepy at work that night, but I made it! And it was worth it.

My sophomore and junior years passed well enough and I was ready for the senior year. The world situation was very uncertain. War was raging in Europe; our young men were being conscripted for military service. What would be next? We wanted to go to Africa as missionaries, not go to war, but we were afraid Leonard would be conscripted. We decided the best course would be to be married and go immediately right to Congo. So we were married on a lovely fall evening, October 10, 1940. After a brief honeymoon in the mountains, we took some trips to raise support. Things were going well.

MARRIAGE

And then I became pregnant! We could hardly go to a faraway jungle with that prospect. Leonard got a job working in an ice cream store, and we found a one-room apartment in Denver and settled down to wait awhile. Our first daughter, Joy, was born that August. She was an infant in my arms when we learned about Pearl Harbor. War with Japan began and this complicated things even more. Just when we thought the situation might get better, I was pregnant again! Fifteen months after Joy, her brother was born. He was such a good baby that we called him Happy though we named him Leonard Leigh. When Joy was three, things were calming down and it looked as though we could soon go.

One of our missionaries in Congo came home because of illness. He recovered and married a DBI graduate who had also just graduated from nurse's training. They were planning to go to Congo right away and thought we could go with them. We gave up our small house, packed up our belongings and set out in our little Terraplane car. We arrived at mission headquarters in St. Louis to complete arrangements.

Then we learned that children were not being issued passports because of the war. Our two children could not go. Leonard was urgently needed on the field, but here we were held up again. I was faced with the crucial decision: should I go with my husband and leave our children behind? Or should I stay with the children and let my husband go without me? Neither prospect seemed good.

I couldn't imagine parents leaving their children behind, though some couples did that. I decided to stay behind. And then the Lord began working things out for us. My almost relatives in San Bernardino, California, offered to care for Joy and Happy. They had no children of their own and were delighted to care for others. I might use this time to good advantage by completing my last year of nurse's training. This was the same place where I had started and the school was willing to let me return. The mission could give us a small income. The pieces were beginning to come together and so I bid my husband a sad farewell, for how long? He went east and we went west, and Joy, Happy and I moved to San Bernardino.

SAN BERNARDINO AND COMPLETION OF TRAINING

The children were soon settled with Hazel and Clarence Stevens and I at the hospital. Their home was quite near the hospital and I could see the children on my free times. It was a hard year for me; I missed my husband and I missed my children. It was difficult to fit into the senior-year program after being out about four years; some sections had to be redone due to differences in the schools' curricu-lums. Finally, I was a graduate nurse! But that was not enough; I had to take the dreaded State Board Exams before I could become an R.N. I will never forget the day I went to Los Angeles for the exam and how strange I felt when it was over. Later, I got the news that I had passed with a good grade. Now it seemed we could go to Congo, but mission affairs moved slowly and it was a full two years between our parting and reunion. My training finished and passports available, it was nec-essary to go to headquarters for final preparations.

ST. LOUIS AND FINAL PREPARATIONS

I was able to buy an old-fashioned wood-burning cook stove at an auction, quite necessary in the jungle. Iron objects were hard to come by because the war required much metal. Other preparations had to be made: immunizations, passports, essential equipment, French lessons, and airfare tickets. We were going on Pan American World Airways. Leonard had purchased our tickets in Congo as the money exchange was better that way. At last, all was ready for us to be on our way. At the last minute, word came from the field that a certain-sized stove-pipe elbow was desperately needed; could I please bring one? One was found, but what could I do with it? Everything had been packed; there was no more room. My grandmother had given me an old-fashioned shopping bag with wooden handles. The pipe just fit. So there I was, off to foreign lands with two small children and a stovepipe in a shopping bag as carryon luggage!

CHILDHOOD AND TEENS

CHILDHOOD AND TEENS

MARRIAGE AND FAMILY

MARRIAGE AND FAMILY

THE PARCELS
"Labourers together with God"
Returning to the Belgian Congo

CHAPTER TWO

ON OUR WAY

The whole mission staff was out to see us off as we boarded the train to New York City. We arrived there early in the morning. A Pan Am agent met us there and took us to the office to confirm our reservations. There it was discovered that we had reservations for only one child. Which one should I leave behind? Neither, of course. Messages were sent between Congo and New York City and the affair was finally straightened out. Of course, Leonard had paid for both of his children. We planned to stay at the Sudan Interior Mission Home until flight time in three days. Immediately, we had to go to the Bronx to get yellow fever shots. I had never ridden a subway before, let alone with two small children, but we got there safely, in time, and back again.

NEW YORK

We had planned an extra, very nice trip to Philadelphia to visit some old friends, the Colgans, who were our Bible teachers back in Tulsa fifteen years before. We had a delightful weekend with them, visiting the zoo and attending church. It was while we were there that we got news that changed all our plans again. The type of plane we were to fly on had had a tragic crash. Consequently, all such planes were grounded indefinitely until full investigation and alterations were made. What could we do then? We went back to New York City and kept in touch with Pan Am, but nothing was available. Our mission said just to wait there, so we moved to New York City.

Fortunately, we could stay on at the mission home. Since we had to wait, we saw some of the sights, but sightseeing with a four- and a three-year-old and no car was difficult. We went several times to Riverside Park which was near, also to the American Museum of Natural History. We went up in the Empire State Building and to a camp on Long Island. I took a few more French lessons and did some sewing, but time passed slowly. I really wasn't too happy with life in the big city. Every few days I phoned Pan Am, but there was no good news.

Finally, after seven weeks, a way opened up. Pan Am was sending a planeload of women and children to Liberia. Their husbands and fathers had been kept there to work in the rubber industry, essential to the war. Now it was safe to let them go to be with these men. Since the load would be women and children, it would have lighter weight than usual, so they could put in extra seats and let us go with them. How happy we were with that news! We were booked to fly late on Sunday evening, so we packed up and another missionary couple took us to LaGuardia Airport. Everything and everybody had to be weighed. About 2:00 a.m. we took off. We were on our way! We had taught the children a variation of a children's song. "We're flying home, we're flying home, to our Daddy over there" ("to our Savior over there"). Now we were really flying.

FLYING

After flying the rest of that night, we spent most of the day at Goose Bay, Labrador, because Gander was fogged in. There was crispness in the northern air. Dinner was at Gander and before long we were out above the Atlantic. Early in the morning we could see the green shores of Ireland. After breakfast at Shannon, we flew to Lisbon, Portugal. Since there had been no scheduled flights for weeks, there were no relief crews along the way. This crew had to make the whole trip, there and back; hence, we had to stop and let them rest. So we spent the night in a good hotel in Lisbon. The children were very tired and sleepy and glad for a bed to sleep in. We had to be up very early the next morning to complete our trip to Africa.

First stop in Africa was Casablanca. I remember seeing, for the first time, the Muslim women, heavily veiled. We refueled and flew over the edge of the Sahara, then on to Monrovia, Liberia. For most, this was the goal of the whole trip. Husbands of these women were waiting at the airport for their families; they had been separated for months. What rejoicing as they greeted their loved ones! In a way, we felt left out but looked forward to our reunion in three or four days.

The whole next day we were the only passengers on that big plane. Has that ever happened since? Though the plane had completed its original task, there were passengers at Kinshasa waiting to return to the USA. That day my children played in the aisle, I read or knitted, and the stewardess took a nap. We were allowed up in the cockpit to view the sky and the land far below. When we crossed the equator, they gave the plane a scary dip to celebrate. Then by late afternoon we landed on Congo soil! We thought we could catch the inland plane and meet Leonard right away, but we were told that there was only one such plane per week and we had just missed this one. What could a woman with two children in a foreign country do? And so we moved in to Kinshasa, Africa.

KINSHASA, CONGO BELGE

At least we could stay at the mission home; there were other missionary families coming or going through there. And so we settled down to wait a week at Kinshasa. It gave us time to adjust to the tropical climate and customs. We took some walks and observed the Congolese going past. It was a long, dreary week, but at last we were headed for the airport to fly to Bukavu. Leonard was already there waiting for us. Someone took us to the airport, but on checking us in, the agent said, "No! You cannot go on this plane!" Well, why not? Our fares had been paid and our papers were in order; what was the hitch this time?

Do you remember the trouble when we arrived in New York City? Pan Am said we had paid for only one child. We thought we had that straightened out, but what the Congo office had done was simply add another child to our bill. Now we must pay for three children! We could not go until that bill was paid. I was completely crushed. Because they had made a mistake, we must suffer. After all the delay already on this trip, this was still more. We must wait another week in Kinshasa and

44

Leonard must wait in Bukavu. After all the difficulties we had already experienced in the two months on the way, the thought of still another week's delay was almost more than I could face! Finally, that week passed too.

So we headed for the airport for the third time. Could we go on this week's plane? Finally, yes! The difficulty had been straightened out. That plane was small and hot; no air-conditioning in a tropical climate, but we did not complain. At least we were on our way! The trip was all the way across Congo, about halfway across Africa. At last, we landed at the international airport at Bujumbura. Bukavu was only a short distance away over a steep mountain range. Then again we landed, this time at Cyangugu, Rwanda. This was the airport for Bukavu as the land was flatter there, and it was only across a small river from Bukavu. Yes! Leonard was there to greet us. He tried to hug all three of us at once. Happiness at last! A joyous reunion; what a joy to be together! The children were a little awed. They were so young when Leonard left that they didn't remember much about Daddy.

LAST LAP OF THE JOURNEY

We spent the night in Cyangugu and the next morning we started out for Ikozi. I would have liked to stay a day and explore Bukavu, but we had to be on our way right then. The reason for this was that the mountain road was one-way, one-way one day and the other way the next. If we waited another day, it would be the time to be coming *to* the city. Leonard had already been gone too long. So we started out on the last lap of our journey on the graveled, narrow, winding, one-way mountain road.

On the way we recounted some of our experiences. Leonard told of his encounter with an official at the airport. He had asked if a woman and two children were booked on the incoming flight. He was told no, but there was to be a woman and three children. Leonard told him his wife had only two children. Then he was asked how long it had been since he had seen me. Leonard replied, "Two years." The agent then asked, "How do you know she doesn't have three?" We took this as a joke. The third one was, of course, the non-existent child I had been erroneously asked to pay for. We laughed about this at the time, but just think how much trouble and grief the mistake had caused us. Probably, with unnecessary hotel bills along the way and other expenses, it would have been cheaper to have bought our tickets in the USA.

After about 100 miles of these twisting, steep mountain roads, both driver and passengers were very weary, the children especially. Though we were not very far from Ikozi, we stayed overnight at a Belgian plantation. Thus, we could arrive at Ikozi about mid-morning. All the station people, whites and Balega, were out to greet us. Betty had taught the Balega ladies to say, in English, "We are happy to see you." That was quite a feat for them. We greeted all the people and told them how happy we were at last to be with them.

After the greetings and some refreshments, Leonard proudly led us to the house he had supervised building for his family. It was quite a large house of poles, sticks, vines and mud with a steep leaf roof. There was a veranda all around the house to protect the mud walls from the rains. The site was dug out of the mountain side and the road ran right by, actually cutting our station in two. The house had a front room, dining room, two bedrooms, an office, kitchen, and bath (not modern). There was also a tiny room behind the fireplace that would do just fine for the younger child. A broad hallway led up to the attic which was finished enough for storage. We felt like it was a mansion. Leonard had been living in a little two-room shack. Now he could move to this big house and live with his family again. And so we moved to Ikozi.

This was a truly amazing adventure, all the way from our west coast to this particular spot in the Congo rainforest. We traveled safely from Los Angeles, St. Louis, New York City, Kinshasa, Bukavu and Ikozi. Though we had plenty of troubles and delays along the way, God was with us. He graciously provided direction, protection, provision and strength. At last, we were at our destination and with husband and father.

CHAPTER THREE

HISTORY AND CUSTOMS

Berean Mission was founded at the Denver Bible Institute in about 1934. Its purpose was to take the message of the Gospel of Jesus to the people of the rainforest of Eastern Congo. It was an interdenominational faith mission. That meant that the missionaries must, by faith, raise their own support. They contacted relatives, friends, churches, and other groups, telling about their work. They hoped many would be interested and give their support, both prayer and financial. Many of our supporters pledged a certain amount each month.

The name Berean was chosen because of a Bible verse, Acts 17:11. The Apostle Paul had traveled as far as Greece, winning believers and starting churches. He faced much opposition, but when he came to the city of Berea, he found the people there receptive and open-minded, searching the Scriptures. At first, the name was Berean African Missionary Society but, after a time, it expanded to Ecuador, Cuba, and Philippines, so the word, African, had to be removed.

As Congo was then under the auspices of Belgium, the Mission needed to know Belgium's policies and work within the rules. The Belgians wanted all missionaries to come to Belgium and take courses in its history and government. Medical people were required to complete a course in tropical medicine. When we first went to Congo, it was during World War II and impossible to go to Belgium, so the government overlooked this at the time.

There were only five people in the first group. They established one station but were soon offered a second site. As the work in Congo grew, we were finally operating in five, widely-spaced areas. After about fifty years, Berean Mission was amalgamated with Unevangelized Fields Mission (UFM). A little later, this mission changed its name to Cross Worlds. It is operating in many areas of the world.

The first step was to apply to Belgium for a concession of territory in Congo where we should work. Another mission, AM, had been granted a large area in the Eastern rainforest. It was much greater than they had any hopes of covering. Mission personnel were happy to have another mission share the work. We took part of their concession. They were very helpful to Berean, even lending a few of their trained young men to help with the language and getting the work started.

As their headquarters was at Shabunda, our state post about three hours drive from our station, we saw them often. As we went there often for mail, business or medical help, we had lots of opportunities for fellowship with them. Many times we had a meal with them. We had a very pleasant relationship with them over the years.

The Balega chief, Songo, was glad to have the mission and helped locate a site. It was atop Musuku Hill. Since the word "musuku" meant light, it was thought an appropriate name for a mission. Missionaries were there to bring the Light of the Gospel to these people. The hill was named Musuku because many musuku trees grew there. These trees exuded a thick flammable sap that, when wrapped in leaves, made good torches.

When Berean personnel arrived, the Belgian government was in the process of building roads through the jungle. They were important for the operation of the mines. A road was being constructed northward through this area and was planned to pass right at the foot of Musuku Hill. At that time, however, the missionaries had to leave their vehicles at the end of the road and walk two or three miles to the station.

All equipment and supplies also had to be carried in by native carriers. The mission paid wages in accordance with the economic situation.

Finally, the missionaries and their equipment arrived and work was begun. Buildings were needed for school, church, workshop and homes. These were built in the native fashion with stick and mud walls and leaf roofs. Workmen were hired to build, bring materials from the jungle, and supply wood and water. The missionaries were busy supervising the work and trying to learn the language, Kilega.

Just a few years later, the mission was offered another site situated on a new road that was being constructed eastward toward Bukavu. This section had been completed and the work crew moved on farther east. That left a number of temporary buildings that the missionaries could use while constructing more durable ones for the mission work. That seemed too good an offer to pass up even though it meant dividing five people between two stations. After praying about it, mission personnel decided to accept this offer.

There were only five original missionaries. Mrs. Beulah Amie had already served a term in Congo under a different mission, so she was the adviser. Miss Amanda Johnson was a graduate of Moody Bible College in Chicago. The other three were Mamie and Albert Jansen, and Irving Lindquist from Denver Bible Institute. Opening the second station would mean three at one station and only two at the other. Mr. Lindquist, Mrs. Amie and Miss Johnson moved to the new station, Ikozi, to begin that work. The Jansens chose to stay at Musuku. So, after only a short time in the area, Berean Mission was operating in two areas.

The Jansens were doing a good work at Musuku. There was church, school for boys, school for girls, and simple medical help available. Everyone was busy; however, they were still waiting for the proposed road to reach them. Then they learned that plans had been changed and the road was taking another route. It would never come near Musuku. It would always be difficult to work so far from a road. To move the whole station to a site on the road seemed more practical. So the search began to find a suitable location.

The Balega knew the jungle and soon located an ideal site. It was on a long, low hill lying parallel to the road. A level area at the top was wide enough for a double row of houses and yards and a central driveway between. There was enough space at one end for a village for the elders, teachers, and workmen and their families. A central area was appropriate for the church and school, workshops, and the medical clinic. Houses for the missionaries would be at the opposite end. The

Belgian government and the Balega people approved, so construction on the new location began.

Building on the new site was off to a good start when personnel changes were necessary. The Jansens went home on furlough; Mamie and Albert Jansen had been working very hard and needed a rest. The construction was left in the hands of Balega workmen with the Christian Balega elders to supervise. That left only three missionaries for two stations. Then Irving Lindquist became very ill with malaria and needed to return home for care. That left only the two women to oversee two stations, so it was good to have Mrs. Amie, an experienced missionary, on the field.

CONGO CUSTOMS

In groups of people, certain customs and standards develop. The customs grow up because these morals work well in the society. We were surprised to learn that many of the customs of the Balega produced a fairly moral and stable society.

RELIGION

Berean Mission was founded in this particular region to teach the people of the Balega tribe. We were especially concerned to find out if they had ideas about a god. If so, what was their name for such a being? We tried to find out about Balega ideas from the past generations. Since our main purpose in being there was to tell about a God of love and His Son, Jesus Christ, one of our first concerns was to identify an appropriate word to use for God. Did they already have a word that denoted an all-powerful, all-wise, holy, loving, divine person? Or should we use our English words and hope to give them the proper meaning? We found that they did have a word that meant a good, super human being, Kalaga.

Yes, they knew that there must be a good and loving god, but they didn't worry about him. He would be kind to them, they thought. What they were concerned about were the bad gods, evil spirits, and souls of their ancestors roaming about the forest. These beings hated people and tried to cause them all kinds of trouble. The Balega believed they made the people ill, caused loss of property, poor harvests, and harm to their children. They were to be feared and appeased, if possible; hence, they had to worship these evil spirits and do what they told them to do. They offered sacrifices, perhaps a chicken, fruit or rice, and they wore certain fetishes or charms to ward off the spirits. They lived in fear.

To be safe, they needed to know what the spirits wanted. A few people seemed to have close contact with these spirits. They became witch doctors, "banganga," who could tell the people what they must do to appease the evil spirits. Witch doctors usually inherited their positions, for such abilities were often handed down from generation to generation. They knew about charms, spells and poisons. The people were in spiritual despair because they did not know that Kalaga was much stronger than the evil ones and would help them if they believed and asked for his help.

It was wonderful to be able to tell them of our God and His provision of salvation and assistance. A number of people did come to the Lord, but many did not understand or were so bound by fear that they hesitated. Beside, why should they believe what these white people from Mputu were telling them? How did they know if what they heard was true? What did these foreigners know about their lives in the forest?

The activities of the witch doctors were not all evil. They knew the jungle trees and plants and how to use them for good purposes as well as bad. Certain plants were good medicine; others had other useful properties. Poisons could be an aid in hunting. Certain plants exuded poison which, smeared on an arrow or spear, stunned an animal so it could be killed and furnish food for the family. Once we were traveling with a group of Balega in the pickup when one cried out for us to stop.

We wondered what could be the matter. We had just passed a patch of a certain plant used for hunting; he seized the opportunity to gather some.

While the Belgians had control, they firmly discouraged the native religion with its worship of fear and spirit appeasement. It was still alive in the hearts of many but was suppressed and hidden from the public. When Congo became independent, these ideas came to the surface. One cult was called Buami. Several groups built their special leaf-covered, long, low huts as special places for their secret meetings. Though they did not agree with the Christians, they did not necessarily try to harm them. To the Christians, it was a potent reminder of the way they used to live. They now had great rejoicing that they had found the way through Jesus and the true and loving God, Kalaga.

AGRICULTURE

In the past, the Congolese had no other resources but what grew in the forest. As other people explored, Indians and Arabs from the east and Europeans from the west, they brought in other plants and crops and taught the people how to raise gardens for food. These crops were rice, peanuts, bananas, plantains, and many kinds of fruit. When we arrived, the Balega were raising their food in small jungle fields. They had devised their own methods of crop rotation and preservation of the forest.

In the early fall, each man cleared his own small field. The men would plant three kinds of food in that field: manioc, bananas or plantain, and rice. These matured at different times and bore some crops for three years. After the last crop was harvested, that piece of ground would not be used again for seven years. A trusted person of each large family group was responsible for assigning specific areas for each family. This was done in cooperation with all the other groups so that one piece of ground would not be used over and over. This was necessary because of the hilly terrain and the tropical climate; almost every afternoon heavy but brief rain poured down. The good soil was washed down the steep hillsides and it took awhile for the fields to be fertile again.

The men did the clearing and planting; the women did the tending and much of the harvesting. Older children helped too when not in school. Boys were to be educated, but girls were to help with the work. It was difficult to persuade people to send their girls to school.

The way they preserved the food they produced was interesting. Many foods needed to be gathered daily, but others, like rice and peanuts, could be hoarded for long periods. From grasses and vines they wove large, sturdy baskets to hold the products. Certain large leaves would be used to line these baskets and cover the tops. Then the baskets would be bound with vine ropes. As long as these certain leaves were around the grain, no insects or rodents invaded those baskets. The natural products of the jungle, plus the crops they were able to grow, provided well for them. They had a good diet, perhaps a little low on protein, but this they remedied by hunting, fishing, and raising chickens and goats.

TRIBAL GOVERNMENT

The Balega were strongly family-oriented. Each extended family group had a chief, usually the oldest male. There were many of such groups in an area which would then have a paramount chief. Our paramount chief was Songo whose village was very close to the mission station. He was friendly and welcomed the mission for he wanted his young men to get an education. Several of his sons studied and worked at Katanti. The Belgian government worked with these chiefs, for they knew the people and their ancient customs.

Though the family groups all belonged to the same tribe, they had little to do with each other because of being isolated in the forest. One of the benefits of Christian teaching was to promote friendship between such groups. Some of our people told us that now members of other groups and even other tribes were their "sisters and brothers in the Lord." One important event occurred later in our work when a fellow of one group married a girl of a neighboring family group. That had seldom happened.

MARRIAGE CUSTOMS

Marriage is an important institution in any social group. Through the years societies have developed their own customs and traditions. The Balega customs were surprisingly good; they promoted morality and protection of women. They were established because they worked well in their society.

The marriage was arranged by the fathers of the bride and groom; however, the young people did have a choice. Girls were important and payment was required for them. The father of the girl set the bride price. He could ask for anything he wished, but it usually was a reasonable commodity for their time and economy. Almost always it involved goats and baskets of cowrie shells, their ancient money. Both were used chiefly for marriage agreements. They no longer used these shells as money; they didn't milk the goats and seldom killed one for meat. The bride's father might ask for lengths of fabric, some cooking utensils, or even an umbrella. When the two fathers finally reached an agreement and the price was paid, the young man was free to take his bride.

The idea of a public ceremony seemed new to them. To promote Christian public witnessing of the marriage was a way of ministry for us. We started a system of premarital counseling for the young couples, encouraging them to be faithful and true to each other, to love and follow the Lord, and to teach their children to love God. It seemed rather crass to reduce marriage to a financial arrangement, but it worked well for the Balega. If the fellow had to pay a good price for her, he was not apt to mistreat her.

This was not the end of the matter, however. Should she become dissatisfied with the arrangement, she might go home to Mama. Then to get her back, the husband had to pay more dowry. He had to try to fix the disagreement also or she would just leave again. She was very valuable; she cooked his meals, gathered firewood, carried water from the spring or river, and worked in the field. When she bore a child, her father could ask for more dowry, for she was now more valuable. It was the same for each subsequent birth. This promoted another custom. When a child was born, he was given a name, often reflecting conditions of the birth (during a storm, for instance). Then when he grew up, married and had a child, he was given a new name, incorporating the name of the child prefixed by the title "Sa" for father, or "Nya" for mother.

Since our daughter Joy was already three years old when Leonard went to Africa, they gave him the name Father of Joy which was "Sakielele." Then mine became "Nyakielele," their word for joy being "kielele."

If the wife died before the husband, he was then required to pay a death tax. When he was already bereft and grieving, it seemed sad to us to have to pay another debt, but it was safety for her. If he had to pay more because of her death, he would not want to injure or kill her. So these customs, strange to us, grew up for the welfare of the family group.

THE BELGIAN GOVERNMENT

Belgium was given custody of the southern part of Congo in the late 1800's. The coalition of European countries supervised conditions and treatment of the native population. This area was rich in valuable minerals, such as gold, silver, copper, iron, wolfram, molybdenum, and even diamonds. Many valuable woods and other products were abundant in the jungles. Soil and climate made possible the growing of tropical fruits, oil palms, cotton, tea, coffee, quinine and peanuts.

Many animals roamed the jungles and grasslands, such as monkeys, chimpanzees, gorillas, baboons, elephants, antelope and wild boars. They were valuable for meat, teeth, ivory, and skins. Any country would be glad to have such resources, but the Congolese people felt that these all belonged to them; it was their country. They owned all this territory but it lay dormant. The Belgians developed mines, farming, some manufacturing, and commerce. Even though the people felt these resources belonged to them, they did not know how to profit by them. Belgium opened these resources to the world and brought many advantages to the Congolese.

The Belgians established government posts at strategic locations. There was only one important post in our area, the small town of Shabunda. Officials were there to oversee relations between the Belgian government and the native people and to maintain control. A sanitary agent was stationed at each post to promote health and sanitary conditions. The Belgians tried to keep peace and reduce crime. They maintained jails for offenders or those who had not paid their taxes. Taxes were used for the good of the country to build and maintain roads and for other benefits.

Guest houses were built at intervals along the roads for these officials to use as they visited each part of the country. Travelers were free to use these shelters as long as the officials were not using them. They contained bed frames and tables but no other furniture or equipment. If a person was to be on the road more than a day, he would need to bring all his necessities with him. A few times we spent a night at one of these just for a change in the routine. Sometimes these officials visited us and we made good friendships.

We stayed at one of these near a mining company headquarters, waiting for our fifth child to be born. The mining company doctor agreed to take my case. We were there over a week until our daughter Melodie was born. We surely appreciated the use of the guest house and the ministrations of the Italian doctor.

The Belgian government encouraged missions, both Catholic and Protestant, to work among the villages. By promoting business enterprises for the Congolese, the government made it possible for them to buy such things as bicycles, sewing machines, cloth, kerosene, lamps, sugar and cooking utensils. The people were happy to obtain such things, but some of them felt that the Belgians were stealing their valuable resources. They did not realize or appreciate all the modern advantages that the Belgians had brought them.

Another way the Belgians aided the Congolese was improved agriculture. They brought in a better grade of rice and encouraged other crops, such as tropical fruits, as well as coffee, tea, peanuts, quinine and cotton. The government promoted more sanitary conditions, requiring each village to move to a fresh location every seven years or so. Quinine was now available to treat the very common malaria, and vaccines were encouraged for polio, yellow fever and small pox. The Belgian government kept law and order by checking periodically on the people. Altogether, the Congolese were much better off under Belgian rule than they have been any time since.

The Balega, in our area at least, seemed to get along quite well with the Belgians. Belgium had given them a new economy. Many could now obtain jobs and earn money; work was available in the mines, on the roads, at the missions, and in the homes of missionaries and Belgians. Those who remained in their villages were needed to produce food and gather forest materials. Thus, almost everyone had a way to earn some money. They could buy a few things at the small rural stores. We liked going down the road to see what our tiny local store had to offer. We usually bought something to encourage the storekeeper.

CONGO ROADS

One of the greatest advantages developed by the Belgians was roads. The Congolese had had only narrow paths through the jungle, permitting only foot travel, so the Belgians built roads all over the country. This was very difficult in our area because of mountainous terrain covered with trees. It was wonderful for us to have even two-way roads to our nearest cities, Kindu on the west on the Congo River, and Bukavu on the east on Lake Kivu. Sometimes it was important to get to our small state post, Shabunda, or to travel between our stations. We greatly appreciated these roads.

The mining corporations were required to offer medical services to their employees and families. Some young Belgian graduate doctors did their internships in Congo. The mining companies provided food, including a certain amount of protein, for their workers. The natural way was for each man to have his own field and raise enough food for his family; however, if a man worked for the mines or roads, he did not have time to raise his own food. To compensate, the companies hired truckers to buy food from the villages and transport it to the mines, so the roads were also very important to the mining companies. They were the means of getting men and equipment to the area and then transporting the mine products so they could be sold.

TRADITIONAL EDUCATION

In the old days, the men of the village gathered in the evenings around a low open fire to visit. They held discussions, reviewed the day's happenings or recounted ancient wisdom; that was their method of education. They told the young people tales of the past over and over until everyone knew them well and could repeat them for younger children. This was learning by rote, the oral method; it was also the way the Balega teachers were teaching children to read. The teachers would read a portion and instruct the children to repeat it over and over until they knew that part very well. The children knew what was on that page, but they could not actually read it.

PROVERBS

The Balega had another way of passing on knowledge by both oral and visual education. It was the use of proverbs or wise sayings. Each proverb became condensed so that two or three words expressed the whole message. For each proverb they made a small object as a reminder. Then they might make a string of such objects and hang them from the eaves before the front door. These were object lessons to help children learn.

The one I liked best was expressed by two words, "Muana, Buato," meaning Child, Boat. The message of this saying was that it takes a long time and a lot of work to shape a tree trunk into a dugout canoe, but when it is finished, it will carry you across the river. Likewise, it takes a long time and a lot of effort to raise a child, but if you do it wisely, that child will care for you when you are old. The emblem for this proverb was a tiny model canoe. When a child saw the object, he or she was reminded of the whole saying and its wisdom.

BALEGA LEADERS

The missionaries realized that they needed help in communicating with these people. Their background, lifestyle and way of thinking were all different from ours; we needed a go-between. We took a few of the wiser, mature, stable men to be our advisers and called them elders. We came to them whenever there were questions involving both parties. They understood the Balega viewpoint and emotional responses; they also had had more contact with white men and could understand both sides.

These men were invaluable and we consulted them often. When these men came to know the Lord, then they not only saw the two human viewpoints but also had the counsel of the Bible and the Holy Spirit to help. Some of them also became spiritual leaders and preachers.

One of these men was quite a bit younger than the others. When we arrived at Ikozi he might have been an older teenager. He had been out to a village teaching when we arrived but came up to our door to greet us. He learned Bible truths quickly and became a Christian; soon he became one of our preachers and evangelists. At the first his name was Ngandu; it became Sasimon when his first son was born.

When we went to Katanti, he went with us. Leonard liked to have him when he went out on evangelistic trips. Once we were going somewhere with the whole family along. We had started early and about noon were tired and hungry. We stopped to rest and eat the lunch we had brought, but not Sasimon. In no time he had gathered a group of the local people and was telling them about the Lord. He really put us to shame and he became a dear friend.

Years later after our retirement in Kansas, Sasimon came to the USA to consult with mission leaders. He visited us in our home and we had a wonderful time. We look forward to visiting with him in heaven.

ANCIENT ABORIGINAL DRESS

OUR LOCAL WITCH DOCTOR – SAKIENSO

BALEGA MISSIONARIES TO ANOTHER GROUP

LEONARD AND BIBLE CLASS

CROSSING LUGULU RIVER BY FERRY

DRIVING ON

DRIVING OFF

POLING OUT FROM SHORE

THRESHING RICE

IRONING WITH THE
CHARCOAL IRON

CHAPTER FOUR
LIFE AT KATANTI

When we arrived in Congo, Berean Mission had two stations, Katanti and Ikozi. Ikozi was the only station operating then so we spent our first year there. I was studying the language, Kilega, and getting used to the people and their lifestyle. I was also helping with medical work at our little dispensary and learning how to run the household with a crew of Balega helpers.

We had been at Ikozi a year when the Jansens returned. They were eager to reopen the work at Katanti. Though the Balega had done remarkably well, much more work was needed. At least the Jansens' house was livable, but the floors were still just dirt. The inside walls were not whitewashed but the house would do for a time. A church building had been erected and a carpenter shop and school building were ready for use.

We were chosen to move to Katanti. The first problem, of course, was a place to live, so Leonard volunteered to go over right away and supervise the building of a house for us. Joy, Happy and I waited at Ikozi. I could help with the dispensary and I sewed curtains for the new house and started Joy's schooling. After about two months, we were very tired of being separated, so the children and I moved to Katanti.

While much progress had been done on our house, it was not possible to live in it yet. A small two-room shed with dirt floor was available and would do for a time. The small front room had space for a bed, a cupboard and a wash stand, and there was one window. The back room was even smaller and quite narrow. The children's beds would not fit, so we devised a bed for the children. A narrow folding army cot with an additional table made it longer. Joy and Happy slept in this one bed, feet to feet. Since we had no facilities for cooking, we had our meals with the Jansens, being very thankful for their hospitality. Of course, this was not a very comfortable arrangement, but we made do until our new house was livable.

I liked this new house very much. There were two windows in most rooms; some were glass and some plastic. We needed the light because of the overhanging roof of the veranda. The floors were slate and easy to keep clean. The ceilings were grass mats tied to the rafters. Storage space in the attic was reached by a good stairway. It was a very good mud house and lasted about fourteen years. This was a record for native-style buildings because rains, dampness and termites did a lot of damage in that climate. This house had a kitchen, pantry, office, dining room, sitting room with fireplace, bath and three bedrooms. A veranda, necessary to protect the mud walls from the rain, was all around the house. It was a happy day when the house was finished; we could move in and live like a family again. We lived in that house the rest of that term and a few times later on. It was our favorite home. Though I did not realize it at the time, many happy years of my life were to be spent at Katanti.

When we were fairly well settled in our new house, we were ready to take our parts in the work of the mission station. Of first importance was the church. By this time we had some trained men who could act as pastors and preachers. Some of the older Balega men helped a great deal with the work of the church. These elder men knew their people and customs and also could better understand their language. While the missionaries taught about God and His Word, the elders helped us understand the people and the people to understand us. We depended on these men and were thankful for them. It was a help that Mamie and Albert Jensen already knew the area though not this particular location.

Mamie Jansen supervised the work with women and girls. She was very good with the Kilega language and did a lot of translation work. One of her projects was translating some of our hymns and gospel songs into Kilega. She was also a musician and taught the people and special groups to sing these songs. The Balega loved music so singing was a valuable part of church services. We had a small pump organ which could be carried about as needed.

Albert Jensen was recognized as the manager of the station. We usually met each week to discuss things and make plans, but Albert was in charge. Among other things, he ran the saw mill which he had been able to bring back with him after their furlough. While there were trees of very good wood all around, it was a lot of work to produce boards for building and furniture. Trees had to be chopped down in the forest and branches removed. Many men were needed to drag trees to the road and load them on the truck which carried them to the saw mill. Some of the men trained for this job became very good carpenters.

The saw mill was a great help. It was powered by gasoline even though gas was very expensive there. Before gas power, workmen would dig a big hole under a felled tree. One man would work from below, one from above. They used a long saw with a handle at each end. By pushing and pulling, they could cut boards but it was a lot of work and not always smooth and straight.

Leonard supervised the workmen in the actual construction of buildings. He also made many trips with the truck to villages where the people harvested supplies from the forest. It might be vines, special leaves or poles; these were needed for the buildings. He paid them by weight for whatever they had collected. Many times Leonard would take a group of elders and students out to the villages, near and far, to hold gospel services. We always had good attendance at these meetings. We were training young men to help with this work which was part of their Bible school training. Balega were a sociable people and liked to get together to visit. Sometimes Leonard took longer trips lasting two weeks or so. A few times I was able to go with him, but usually this did not work out.

My work was the medical department. At first I worked from a small shed with a table and a box for a cupboard. I began treating wounds, ulcers, intestinal parasites, fevers and infections. Some of the Balega women helped with births. When we needed something sterile or very clean, I boiled it on the stove or if it were cloth, ironed or baked it. I mixed liniments, ointments and potions from bulk supplies. We filled capsules with quinine powder for malaria. Many times I would be called to handle an emergency. At first I would be very tense and nervous, wondering what would be required. Later, I learned to be calmer about the situation.

Late one evening some men carried in, on a homemade litter, a man who had just received a deep spear wound in his chest. It was a miracle that the lungs, heart, blood vessels and nerves had not been injured. In those early days, Katanti had very little equipment to work with or any place to care for patients. We put him down on the ground and built a little fire to keep him warm. Of course the spear had been dirty and his skin not too clean. I very gently tried to cleanse the wound, being afraid I would do further injury. This was before antibiotics; I sprinkled in some sulfa powder, applied a clean dressing, and gave him some aspirin for the pain.

We watched him very carefully and he survived the night. A Balega family on the station took him into their home, but the only place they had for him was a grass mat and room for a bed on the earthen floor. In a few days he was healing well. One day I went to change his dressing. As I passed the foot of the bed, a duck nipped me on the leg. I was a bit startled. The people frequently kept animals in the house to prevent thefts or to keep the animals from wandering away. No doubt they intended to eat that duck.

We were curious to know how he had received such a serious wound. There had been a village gathering and the brother of the wounded man, Sakamunzila, was in the group. A man was very angry with this brother and came at him with his spear. Sakamunzila saw the danger and placed himself between the spear and his brother, thus saving his brother's life but putting his own life in grave danger. This made a wonderful spiritual lesson for the people. Jesus gave His life to save us from sin. He placed himself between us and the terrible death penalty for sin.

We made good progress that first year, keeping up with the church, five grades of school, a small medical service, and evangelistic outreach to the villages. Three new missionaries arrived. They were especially interested in the school for the Balega. When the children finished five grades, they thought they were well-educated. And they were, according to their standards and opportunities; however, they had no idea how very much more there was to learn.

To teach more grades, we needed more school buildings and homes for the newcomers. One new missionary lived with us until the new home was ready. We tried different methods and materials in the attempts to construct better and more durable buildings quickly. There were always such projects going on. We tried sun-dried mud blocks for some. The trouble with that was that sheds must also be built to shelter the drying blocks from our frequent rains. Nevertheless, two new mud block school buildings were constructed which lasted several years. The difficulty of the native style, using poles, vines, sticks, leaves and mud, was the ever-present attacks of termites, eating away the wood parts. Mud blocks avoided this but were more vulnerable to the rains.

Managing a home with a crew of Congo helpers was a learning experience for me. We had a cook and helper, a cleaner and a laundry fellow. Not having to do the housework gave me more time for other work. I was teaching our children, training medical helpers, and teaching some classes in the Balega school. Most of the classes were for boys only, as the Balega felt that girls should stay home and work. They also thought that girls were incapable of learning much.

Our daughter Joy was six and had started first grade before our move so I taught her part of each morning. Our son Happy was not quite ready for school but listened and played nearby. Leonard would be at the Balega school.

Keeping five grades of school going was very important. The people were very proud to have a school nearby to educate their children. Each of us missionaries did a part of the work in the school. Leonard taught Belgian history and geography (required by the government). I taught basic hygiene and trained a few special fellows to do the simpler work at the dispensary. Some had received previous training; soon I had a group of quite capable helpers.

I taught simple hygiene, especially stressing the value of frequent hand washing. Later, I wondered just how they could manage it. They had no running water, no inside bath facilities, probably no pitchers, no wash bowls and no towels. Washing hands meant walking down a steep, slippery hill to the spring. They were not likely to do this several times a day.

I taught the fellows some simple sewing, how to patch a tear in a garment, and how to make a buttonhole. A few fellows had obtained Singer sewing machines which they operated by turning the wheel with the right hand and guiding the sewing with the left. They knew how to make shorts, shirts and women's tops. They did quite good work except for buttonholes. They just cut slits which soon began to tear, so I taught them how to make good buttonholes. I also taught them to knit and one fellow began knitting socks. Then I taught a group of women simple sewing. One project was a pillow and pillowcase; they stuffed the pillows with dried grass. They were amazed to learn that one could make cases that could easily be removed for washing.

The medical work was increasing. Beside treating diseases, we also tried to teach ways to stay well. We had a baby clinic on a special day every week to see if the young children were progressing well. Many of the toddlers wore nothing except a light rope about the loins. On this rope were hung various ornaments or fetishes to keep the evil spirits from harming them. They would use all sorts of such charms; one child had simply a padlock on his loin string. We were teaching them that our God was far stronger than the evil spirits and could protect them much better. If they trusted in the Lord, they would not need these fetishes; they would no longer have to put these things on their children. I knew that many mothers would just remove these when they came up the mission road and then put them on again as they left, but some were taking the great step of faith in the Lord Jesus Christ and not using the charms.

DAILY SCHEDULE

On a usual day we were awakened by drumbeats calling the people to devotions with which Leonard usually helped; the cook began breakfast. Later, I consulted with my cook about meals for the day and then began school for Joy. Leonard was already at the station school. About mid-morning Leonard came home to teach our children and I went to my classes at the school. We often had a lemonade break in between these activities.

After lunch we all had a siesta during the hottest part of the day. Then school and building work was resumed. There was then time for behind-the-scenes activities such as preparing for classes, overseeing housework, writing and answering correspondence, sterilizing dressings and instruments for the dispensary, and preparing medicines. I had a recipe book for medicines just as we had recipes for food.

The evening meal was served early because, at the equator, days and nights are twelve hours each the year around. The dark comes early and quickly. After the meal, we gathered in the parlor for evening devotions with our family. While we were reading and praying, our house helpers cleaned up the kitchen and finished the day's work. Then they all marched past to say "Segala busoga" (good night; rest well) and went home to their families.

We usually had some lighter tasks to finish. We used kerosene lamps for our lighting, although later, for a time, we had a gasoline generator to power lights for a short period in the evening. Then it was bedtime. We had to be sure our mosquito nets were tucked in all around to escape insect bites and malaria. Even though we were just about 100 miles south of the equator, we had comfortably cool nights and usually used light blankets. So thus a day passed at Katanti Mission Station in the rainforest in Congo, Africa.

REST AND RECREATION

We had some opportunities for breaks in the routine. Sometimes we visited other stations and sometimes our small state post, Shabunda, for business or medical help. While there, we visited our friends at their station. On rare occasions we went to one of our cities, Kindu to the west and Bukavu to the east, for business, shopping, or just a change from the forest. We had good friends, the Adamsons, at Kibagora, a station on a hill overlooking Lake Kivu. We had good times there and enjoyed the beautiful view.

We always looked forward to annual conferences of all the Berean missionaries; alternate stations served as hosts. It was fun to visit other stations but also interesting to be the host station. Beds had to be found for a number of guests for several nights, and meals had to be planned and supplies on hand. Schedules had to be arranged. Somehow or other, things usually went smoothly. There would be station reports, mission business, plans for the future, and much discussion, prayer, and mutual encouragement. There would also be times of fellowship and fun.

Occasionally, missionaries from other mission groups would stop by or some Belgians would visit. Once, a couple from another mission stayed with us several days. There had been extra heavy rains and our nearby river, the Lugulu, had risen five or six feet. The ferry was unable to cross, so there was nothing for them to do but wait until the waters went down. We were glad for their company.

Even though it might seem monotonous, there was always something interesting going on. There were the Sunday church services when people came from surrounding villages. Often a group of us would go on bicycles to hold children's services in some village along the road. If nothing else, we could always go for a walk in the jungle which was all about us. We never tried this without a Mulega along, for one could easily get lost or encounter dangers. We followed forest paths which had been cut by machetes through the thick vegetation. Almost every afternoon we would have a brief but heavy rain, especially during our winter rainy season; that is, during our winter in the USA, it was mid-summer there, the hottest part of the year.

At night we could take a walk and gaze at the Southern Cross and other constellations in the southern sky. Leonard and I called these evening strolls our "moonlight walks." One evening Joy told us she wanted to go for a "moon walk"; though she should have been in bed, we let her go with us that time.

A VISIT OF THE ANTS

In the forest there were both large animals and small enemies, such as insects. We learned to watch out for these dangers. One night I felt something crawling over my shoulder. I realized it was an army of ants. I quickly woke the children and told them to grab a pillow and blanket. We all hurried over to our neighbor's house which was not locked. We spent the rest of the night on their front room floor. Were our hosts surprised to find that uninvited guests had moved in during the night? The ants were uninvited guests at our house too. It was useless to try to fight these ants. They were everywhere in a second, some even dropping down from the ceiling. It was best just to leave. As they marched through the home, they repaid our hospitality by cleaning out all harmful insects, roaches and rodents, leaving a clean house.

The children and I had another experience with these ants soon after our arrival in Congo. We had gone on a walk at the edge of the jungle when, suddenly, the ground was covered with ants. What could I do with two children? I grabbed up Happy, telling Joy to stay right there, and carried him out of the insects. Then I ran right back and carried Joy out. We then picked off any ants that had come with us. They really hold on tightly, sometimes even letting their heads be torn off. We learned not to go on jungle paths alone and to watch for columns of ants marching along. If they were not disturbed, they would stay in their column and cause no trouble, marching right on. At one point, we were raising rabbits and their pen was on the veranda. Someone saw ants approaching. We knew they would eat the rabbits, so we discouraged them with firebrands and they chose another route. Oh, the adventures in the jungle!

CHRISTMAS AT KATANTI

Christmas at Katanti was always a special time. Hopefully, some missionary barrels had arrived with gifts for the children. (Mail was often delayed and once we celebrated Christmas in March.) The important celebration for Christmas was the annual conference for the Balega.

The Balega came from all the surrounding country, some walking through the forest a day or more. The mining companies shut down, allowing their employees to come. The population on the station increased about 100 percent. The Katanti Balega gladly made room for the guests in their homes somehow, but enough food was another problem. The week before, our missionary men would go out to the villages and collect all the surplus food. Usually this was a gift from the Christians. This surplus was then hauled back to the station and reserved for the visitors. Those walking a long way would not be able to carry much extra food, but this way there was plenty for all.

For the celebrations, special meetings were planned for two or three days. There were services in early morning, late morning, mid-afternoon and evening, and special classes for the children, women and men. There would be lots of singing, and sometimes there would be a new translation of some of our Christmas songs. Mamie had translated many songs, and Betty Lindquist did a good translation of "O Little Town of Bethlehem." Though I was not fluent in Kilega, I managed to arrange two Christmas songs, "There's a Song in the Air" and "Dear Little Stranger." The Balega loved to sing these and many other Christian songs. One year, the carpenters made a little manger for the children's special program. After that, we used that crib in the maternity room for newborn babies.

One year there was a terrible windstorm just a few days before Christmas. It blew the roof off of the church building and did a lot of other damage, and there was no time to rebuild. We were all concerned about the conference; we could not cancel the celebrations. We moved the church benches and extra chairs to a flat area near the church and held the services outside. It really went quite well. Later, we learned that an epidemic of polio was spreading through our country. It is possible that some of our people would have contracted the disease if we had held the services with the people packed inside the church building.

Special offerings would be given at these celebrations. These might consist of an egg, a torch of musuku, a bunch of bananas, plantains, other fruit, some rice, or whatever else the people wished to give to the Lord. The missionaries would buy the food items from the donors and that money would go into the church funds. The Balega had an interesting way of counting the attendance. They took palm leaves and gave a small frond to each person who came. As the service was dismissed, the ushers collected these fronds which could easily be counted.

So at Christmas we all had a wonderful time, singing together, worshiping God, and thanking Him for the gift of His Son, the Babe of Bethlehem. Then it would be sad for the visitors to leave. These conferences were happy times for both the Congolese and the missionaries.

We had spent only a short time at Ikozi before it was our first Christmas time. There were our two children, the Lindquist baby Jimmie, a one-year-old, three women and two men. Just before

Christmas, we had a bad storm that hemmed us in on both sides by landslides. There were no shopping trips, no mail, no phone calls, but we had a great time. We exchanged gifts, small things we had made from what we happened to have. We had a feast and celebration together. There were also special services at the church for the station Balega and all the villagers who were able to come.

When conferences were over, then we would have our family Christmas. We put up what decorations we had. Flowers and greenery were plentiful. Though there were many trees, there was not anything like a Christmas tree. I innovated by taking several palm leaves, stripping off the fronds on one side of each leaf, and then binding the ribs together to make a sturdy trunk. This made a fairly good tree except that the fronds were very flexible and could hold up only very light decorations. We either made gifts or hoarded appropriate items for months ahead of time. We always hoped mail or packages from the USA would arrive before Christmas. With what we had on hand, we always had good family and station celebrations.

We would have a special meal of chicken or wild game, rice, and greens or canned or fresh vegetables. For dessert, our Balega cooks went all out to produce special treats. They baked cookies, cake, pie or pudding. Usually fruit was plentiful.

Sometimes we would have a feast for all the station missionaries; other times we preferred to have the time just as families. A few times we had potluck with all our Balega friends. We felt bad to be eating the food they had worked so hard to produce, but they were delighted to share with us. We usually brought cookies, for that was a special treat for them. What they liked best from us was plenty of warm tea with lots of sugar. Though not as plentiful as Christmas in the USA, we all had a joyous time celebrating God's great gift to the world, Jesus the Messiah, our Savior, God's Son.

Most of our African Christmases were spent at Katanti, but one was while we were refugees at Muyebe with Burundi people. I especially remember that very early Christmas morning. Carolers came by singing beautiful Christmas songs. There I learned the Kirundi words to our song "Shepherds We Have Heard on High." I still know those Kirundi words.

Our family life was very pleasant. I was so happy to be with my husband again and for the children to be with their father. At the time Betty Lindquist was due to deliver her second child. A Belgian doctor came a few days early and was there for the delivery. They asked us to come so I could be the nurse for Betty. While I was there, I discovered that I was pregnant; I experienced a strong episode of morning sickness. I was miserable but did manage to help when Tom was born. Sadly, after about three months, I lost that baby. A Belgian doctor drove out from Shabunda, our state post, to care for me and possibly saved my life. We all four were very sad at this loss.

I had always wanted a large family, having been raised by my grandparents as an only child and having missed my siblings. So I was really happy when our third child was on the way. When Joy was nearly nine, we did have a baby girl, Merry Sue. She was born in the very small mining company hospital at our state post. Our Balega women were especially excited about the birth of the new baby. Everyone in the area wanted to come see the new white baby. She was only two months old when it was time for our first furlough.

OUR MUD HOUSE AT KATANTI & SON "HAPPY"

JUNGLE HILL TOP

PUTTING ON LEAF ROOF

VILLAGE MEETING

BABY CLINIC

BALEGA (PRECIOUS) CHILDREN

CHAPTER FIVE

FIRST TRIP HOME

Time for our first furlough came. Leonard had been on the field six years but I only four. The usual term was five years but Leonard had already passed that, so we compromised with a year extra for him, a year less for me. In 1950 we had made arrangements to fly home on a plane owned by another mission. We were to meet that plane at the Congo capital city, Leopoldville (Kinshasa). As we touched down at our first stop, a tire blew out, nearly wrecking the plane. We were quite frightened but all were safe. We had to wait most of the day until a new tire could be flown in.

Finally, we reached Kinshasa; however, the mission plane was delayed as a crew member was sick. We waited several days. Then

Leonard learned of a ship sailing from the Congo port, a day's train trip from the capital. We were about halfway there when a message reached us that the plane would be ready the next day. So we got off the train and waited in a small station for this same train to pick us up on its return trip. The worst part of this trip was that Joy was sick with a fever and felt miserable all the way. We were relieved that she was much better the next day.

Our plane, a converted army bomber, arrived and we were all ready to go though were amused when we saw the crew. Since this was not a commercial flight, the crew did not have to wear official uniforms. They were each wearing a brightly-colored African-style shirt bought in Congo. We boarded the plane and found our places. At the beginning, we were to ride in the section that had been the bomb bay. We soon took off and flew first to Liberia and then across the South Atlantic to Brazil.

We spent that night at an army barracks in Natal. The next day we took a thrilling flight over the jungle and the Amazon Delta. We were soon over the Caribbean, landing on the island of Trinidad. That night we stayed at a nice hotel and had corn flakes and real milk for breakfast. Trinidad had been an English colony so cars there drove on the left side of the road. After our years in the Congo where cars traveled about ten miles an hour, it seemed that the cars were going very fast and on the wrong side of the street! We were frightened at first.

This trip had not been easy so far with the accident and delays, not to mention that I was caring for a small baby, but the worst was yet to come! From Trinidad we were flying over the Caribbean toward Puerto Rico when, all at once, there was smoke in the cabin. While the engineers were investigating the trouble, the attendant passed out life jackets. I looked down at the sea and wondered how I could jump into the water with my baby in my arms. The crew soon discovered that a super charger had overheated. The problem was remedied by simply cutting off that super charger and the danger was averted. This meant, however, that we were required to fly lower in order to get enough oxygen.

After going through customs at San Juan, Puerto Rico, we flew toward the good old USA. We were scheduled to spend the night in Florida, but as a hurricane was brewing over the Gulf, the crew decided to proceed on to the mission headquarters at Springfield, Missouri. Can you imagine the joy and relief we felt to be on the ground, safely back in our homeland?

A problem developed our first night in the USA. Where could we put the baby for the night? The room we were given contained an empty dresser. We put a drawer on the floor, padded it with blankets, and she had a safe crib for the night. A missionary couple met us and the next day drove us to St. Louis to our own mission headquarters. We were home!

FIRST FURLOUGH

Some folks think that a furlough is a time of rest for missionaries. A more accurate expression might be "home assignment." The missionary at home had the responsibility of reporting the affairs and progress on the field and seeking to interest and inspire new contacts to pray and give for the work. It would be great if he could enlist others to be missionaries also. Usually there was the task of raising more personal and mission financial support. Inevitably, some of those who had pledged support were no longer able to do so or had died. In our case, our family had increased by another child, and the older ones now had greater expenses for school and clothes.

Our first three months were spent at the mission headquarters in St. Louis with a couple of easy trips to visit churches. Then we began a trip of about four months. As it was then very early spring, we went south first to Texas, New Mexico, Arizona and California. We met many good friends and visited churches on the way. Also, both Leonard and

I had relatives near the west coast to visit. (Though they bewailed our going so far away as Africa, we probably would not have seen them any more frequently if we had remained in the States.)

We loved the area around San Francisco with the Golden Gate Bridge, Muir Woods, and beautiful flowers everywhere. While we stayed there, the baby had a light case of the measles, but the Lord protected us in that there were no complications. I did not feel well all this trip due to being pregnant with our fourth child. From there we drove north and had a grand time in Oregon and Washington, visiting friends and especially my mother and several siblings and their families. We had a number of friends from DBI in Montana and Wyoming; it was good visiting them and their families and churches.

Finally, we reached North Platte, Nebraska. Since Leonard had grown up in this area, we had lots of friends there. Also, one of our classmates had helped start a church there and pastored it for many years. We designated it as our home church. The people there provided a home for us which we appreciated very much. Then we spent a short time in Denver where our fourth child, Ruth Gay, was born in August 1951. We returned to North Platte for the rest of our furlough.

It was always amazing to me how Leonard was able to do all the planning, make all the arrangements, reservations and connections, figure schedules, and arrange provisions along the way. In our career, however, he had to do this many times and often with much more complicated situations.

CHAPTER SIX

LIFE AND STUDIES
IN BELGIUM

Our second term began with our departure from North Platte in 1952, though it would take a year before we arrived in Congo. This term would take us to three continents and across three seas. We were going to Belgium for more training. We started out driving with a tiny baby and a toddler. Joy, Len and Merry Sue rode in the back seat, and Leonard and I and the baby in the front. We stopped briefly at our headquarters in St. Louis; then we were on our way to New York City. Leonard did very well driving in big city traffic. We spent that night in a small hotel in Harlem. We were all hungry so Leonard went out to find some food. He was apprehensive about walking the streets of Harlem at night, but he brought back food and all was well.

Leonard had arranged for passage on a certain ship, but on our arrival we were told that the ship would be unable to sail as scheduled. He found places, however, on a Holland-American ship that was departing in three days, but the only accommodations left were first class. Should a humble missionary family sail first class? We had our choice: sit and wait and pay hotel bills, or sail right away first class. It seemed more reasonable to us to be on our way, so we went first class.

Since we had flown both ways before, it was another adventure to go by ship this time. We landed in Holland just in time for their Tulip Festival and celebration of the Queen's birthday. We spent a day on a bus trip to see the millions of flowers and also the North Sea. Unfortunately, no one on that bus spoke either English or French so we missed a lot of explanation. That evening we took a train to Brussels, Belgium. We had places at a Belgian mission home for a few days while we looked for a permanent apartment.

We went to Belgium to get more training. Leonard needed to study more French and take a course on Belgian history and government policies. Belgium, being the mother country of the Congo, required us to understand her method of governance. I needed training since Belgium required nurses to complete a yearlong course in tropical medicine in order to conduct medical services in the Congo.

This training in Belgium necessitated our finding a dwelling, schools for the children, and a means of transportation. We had shipped our passenger car there, so that would help with getting about.

We soon found a small ground-floor apartment with two rooms, kitchen and bath that would meet our needs. A big old gas cook stove was in the kitchen, and bath water was heated by a small unit which hung on the bathroom wall. It only worked when we turned on the hot water faucet. The rooms were heated by an oil heater in the middle room. In the cold weather, we kept the front room closed to preserve heat. There was a long, narrow backyard where the children could play. There were a few small fruit trees which we were free to harvest. This was in a good neighborhood near the Botanical Gardens, the Basilica, and a streetcar line.

The problem of the children's schools was soon solved. Both the boys' and the girls' schools were nearby. Joy's was a little farther but not too far to walk. Hap's school also had a nursery where Merry Sue, who was nearly two, could be cared for. Her brother could be responsible for her. These schools taught only in French which was quite an adjustment for Joy and Happy, but they got along quite well. All

Belgian girls were taught to knit at an early age. They were required to knit a project at school. I had taught Joy to knit but she had not practiced much and she could not knit nearly as fast as the other girls. Thus, her teacher was always encouraging her to "tricot" (knit).

Our housing and schooling arrangements left the baby, Gay, at home with Leonard, but he would often have to be away for classes and shopping. We hired a Belgian maid to help with the housework and care for the baby. She took good care of Gay and even knitted a little sweater for her to protect her chest from the cold; it was called a "cache couer" (hide your heart). She brought her lunch each day, a "tartine" (sandwich) and gave half to Gay because Gay liked the Belgian bread. We invited her to eat with us, but she felt that a maid should not dine with her employers. Additionally, the occupants on the ground floor were required to keep the sidewalk in front of their apartments spotless. She did this for us as well.

Everything seemed to be cared for. We settled down to life in our European city. I still had a problem, though. My medical training was offered at the Prince Leopold Institute of Medicine Tropical in Antwerp. This required my living away from Leonard and the family during the week. On Saturdays I could take the train back to Brussels for a little time with my family. Then Monday mornings I could go back to Antwerp in time for classes. We could have chosen to live in Antwerp except that the language there was Flemish, a somewhat Germanic tongue. In Brussels, French is the legal language. We felt it would be more profitable for the children to learn French.

We soon found a place for me in Antwerp in the home of a couple who operated a photo shop. I had to pass through the studio to get to the back stairs to my room. The winter there was cold and gloomy. Once the weather was made even more miserable by a storm over the North Sea. The wind was continuous and so strong that it drove flooding sea waters clear up the river to Antwerp. My room was always cold in spite of an oil heater. Consequently, I often studied with all my outer clothes on and a sweater, bathrobe, lap robe and double socks. Still, my fingers and nose were very cold, but I survived.

Two English missionary girls stayed in the same apartment in Antwerp. They also were taking the tropical medicine course. I enjoyed their companionship as we walked together to school which was not too far away. One of these missionaries had to leave her husband and small daughter in England for the duration of the course. Our hosts were very kind to us and, in spite of their language being Flemish, used French when we were around to help us improve our language skills. This was a blessing since all of our classes were in French.

A number of other missionaries from various countries also attended classes in Belgium. On Sunday afternoons once a month we all got together for Christian services and mutual encouragement, and did we ever need that! It was helpful to fellowship with missionaries of other missions and countries since we all had the same goal, missionary work in Congo.

Christmas in Antwerp was a special time. In typical European style, the celebration began on December sixth and was observed with several other special days. Some of their customs were different, but they truly celebrated the birth of our Savior Jesus. The stores were beautifully decorated with many displays of toys, gifts, and the famous Belgian chocolates.

Our Antwerp hosts made our Christmas celebration a happy and interesting occasion. They invited my husband and children to come for the celebration. The food was delicious. Madame even made two darling little blue crepe dresses, one for Merry Sue and one for the little English daughter. How very sweet of her to do that. I had managed to make a few small things for the children and bought a few toys also. One was a nice play set of aluminum cooking pans for Joy. She still has one of the little pots. We enjoyed a few days together as a family. Our missionary group gave a Christmas concert as part of our celebration.

After a short vacation, our classes resumed. We had heard from former students that the course was tough. The material was complex to start with and studying it in French added to the complexity. Beside anatomy and the usual tropical diseases and treatments, we studied tropical insects and intestinal parasites. This required quite lot of study under the microscope.

We all studied hard and did a lot of praying. We were anxious, knowing that exam time would soon be upon us. We also knew that our future in Africa depended on our passing this course.

Each area of our studies had a different exam. Some were one-to-one oral questions and answers. I'm sure in these my examiner had to overlook my inadequate French and concentrate on the content. Other parts required knowing the identity of tropical insects and micro-scopic identification of eggs of various parasites. I did fairly well on most of the exams and was the first student to complete the microscopic part. What a relief that was because I had not done well in practice. I'm sure the Lord helped me.

Some months passed and Merry Sue was adapting well to nursery school. She celebrated her second birthday on which we gave her a pair of wooden shoes. Joy and Happy were keeping up with their classes, all in French, and baby Gay was well cared for.

I was learning a lot in school and felt I had received excellent preparation for the diseases we would encounter in the tropics. Leonard had done well also, caring for the family, taking French classes and studying. During our stay we had learned our way around Brussels and Antwerp. We were able to visit some old castles, forts and museums. We saw famous art pieces and one of the earliest printing presses. We would have liked to explore more, but we were there for business, not pleasure, and on a limited budget.

Finally, the school term was over and exams taken. The exams were followed by a formal convocation to announce final grades. All three of us missionaries had passed! Praise the Lord! So our time in Belgium was at an end. We packed up all our belongings and headed for Africa.

The experience had been interesting and profitable, but also very stressful and tiring. We were glad to have some free time and also to leave the cold, gloomy winter weather of that country. We were looking forward to some African sunshine.

CHAPTER SEVEN

VOYAGE & VACATION

As we left Brussels and drove through the country, little Merry Sue kept saying, "Wanna see a oiseau." As this was very early spring and still cold, we were not apt to see birds, but it showed that she had learned some French.

We spent the first night in Luxemburg, then on into the mountains of Switzerland. There we visited a good friend that Leonard had met during his time in Portugal, Mr. Georges Andre. We met his family and then visited a Swiss Bible school, Emmaus, in the mountains. We also visited the Castle of Chilon. Next, we drove through southern France, viewing the Alps in the distance. We were headed to Marseille, a busy French port on the Mediterranean.

It was already quite warm in southern France. We no longer wanted our warm winter coats and surely would not need them in Africa. We gave them to a mission that helped Gypsies. There we met our ship, the Durban Castle, which had started from England. We had taken our car to Belgium where it had been a great help. Now we were taking it to Africa. However, the hold of the ship was apparently already full of cars, so ours was anchored out on the deck with a tarp to protect it.

The first stop was Genoa, the home of Columbus. Here we bought an Italian accordion to help with music at Katanti church (if I learned to play it). We sailed down the west coast of Italy, passed between Italy and Sicily, and saw the glow from Mt. Etna. Crossing the Mediterranean was a bit rough and everyone got seasick, but we landed safely at Port Said where Leonard bought a good leather briefcase, probably of camel hide.

SAILING THE SUEZ CANAL

Near Port Said we entered the Suez Canal. It was thrilling to think of all the work to cut this waterway between Asia and Africa. It was just about wide enough for one ship at a time. At that time Joy lost a baby tooth. We threw it in the canal to celebrate. There it still rests on the sandy bottom. The canal ends at the city of Suez. There we were furnished a ride on a glass-bottomed boat. We could view the passing fish and all kinds of water life.

Then we came to Aden, Arabia. After descending from the side of the ship on a rope ladder, we were taken to the land in a small boat. There we saw a camel caravan and rode a camel cart through a mountain tunnel. Also, we saw cisterns that, supposedly, King Solomon had devised for the Queen of Sheba. They were small at the bottom, so if the water was scarce, it would be deep enough to dip the buckets in. Then they expanded, step by step, to accommodate more water. They must have been great help in that desert country. We enjoyed some Arabian food and then sailed back across the bay in the small boat to the ship. We climbed the ship's ladder and arrived safely back on board.

From Aden we entered the Indian Ocean and sailed south down Africa's east coast. On the way we crossed the equator. The ship's crew held a grand ceremony and celebration. It was an old custom to celebrate when crossing the equator. It is still a custom on ships and airplanes. Our first port in Africa was Mombasa, Kenya, which was very hot. Since our car had not been put in the hold but anchored on deck, it was no problem to have it unloaded. The idea of spending a night in a motel on the beautiful white sand beach seemed much more inviting than spending another night on the sweltering ship deck. Our long voyage was over. From Mombasa, we drove down the coast to Dar-Es-Salaam, Tanzania.

Here we turned west, boarding the train across Tanzania to the end of the line. This is quite a special railroad, reaching nearly halfway across Africa. The railroad ends at Rugigi. Here is where Stanley finally found Livingston. He greeted Livingston with the words, "Doctor Livingstone, I presume." Since they were the only white men in that part of Africa, it was an amusing statement. I well remember this trip and it was an uncomfortable night. The road was often rough and the train kept swinging from side to side. For the evening meal we were served soup and soon discovered ants in the soup. We three older ones tried to scoop the ants out of the soup of the younger ones as well as our own. The train kept on swinging and we had a hard time getting any nourishment.

Older missionaries like to tell this joke. A quite new worker finds ants in his soup. He calls the waiter and complains, insisting that the soup be thrown out and clean soup in a clean bowl be brought. When a missionary who has returned for a second term finds ants in his soup, he fishes out the ants and eats the soup. By the third term, he shouts, "Oh boy, protein," and eats the soup, ants and all.

Our car had come on the same train, so now we had our own transportation for the rest of the trip. We had traveled east, south and west; now we would be going north. We drove up the east side of Lake Tanganyika to Bujumbura. There we began to feel more at home. Our city, Bukavu, was only about 100 miles north.

We had another adventure on this trip north. It was very swampy near the east edge of the lake. A branch railroad had been built up on an embankment, and this elevation was just a bit wider than the tracks. An automobile road also had to go on this embankment, so a car would travel with one wheel between the tracks and the other on the narrow edge beside the tracks. There was radio connection between the ends of this stretch to assure that traffic was one-way and safe. When we reached this point, the radio was not working well so our signal did not get through. After we had waited for some time, the radio operator said that there was never a train coming our way at this time of day. It would be perfectly safe to proceed. We were a bit apprehensive but we started, carefully watching the tracks ahead. What could we have done if a train did come our way? You may be sure we were very relieved when we safely reached the end of that section.

Our road was mostly north toward Bukavu. There was quite a mountain range between the two cities with a narrow twisting road climbing up the escarpment. The road was just wide enough for one-way traffic. To avoid collisions, road blocks were set up at frequent intervals and each station was equipped with a large drum. When a car entered a section, the drummer would send the message to the next station. An oncoming car would not be permitted to enter that section until the first car reached the next station. The drummer would then send an all-clear signal back to the first station. So we crossed the mountain pass and safely arrived back in our own territory and our city, Bukavu.

After spending the night in Bukavu, we set out on the final leg of our journey. This way was also a twisting, up-and-down narrow mountain road through the forest. Much of it was regulated as a one-way road but this stretch was managed differently. One could go one direction on certain days and the other way on the other days. The drive from Bukavu to Ikozi takes most of a day and is quite tiring. We were very weary when we arrived at our station, Ikozi, and were home again. Our Balega friends came to greet us and sing their version of the welcome song. It was really quite moving to be back with them again.

TIME AT IKOZI

Back at Ikozi we moved into a rather new brick house which had been readied for us. Most of our furniture and possessions had been stored at Katanti, so arrangements were made to get our things because we would be staying at Ikozi for awhile. The beginning of a small school for missionary children had been started at Katanti. There were only six or seven scholars at that time. We sent Joy and Happy there for school; they were in fifth and fourth grades, respectively. It was very hard to leave them there, though we knew they were with good friends and teachers. Merry and Gay were not yet school age.

We tried to enter into the work there. I helped some in the dispensary and school. Leonard and the other men always had work, teaching, preaching, hauling, and building. We both were nearly exhausted, however. We had experienced a frightening trip home, a long deputation trip with a baby, and then the birth of another baby. After that came the intensive study in Belgium and the tiring trip to Ikozi. After a few months at Ikozi, we decided that we should take a month's vacation. We really should have done this before leaving Europe. We were tired of cold, gloomy Belgium and longed for African sunshine.

VACATION

We had traded in our sedan car for a Studebaker pickup. A sturdier vehicle was needed for our rugged country. The Balega called it "stu de bakay." Leonard had constructed another seat back of the front seat where two or three children could ride. We also managed a canvas cover to protect from the rain. We prepared for a long trip and loaded our pickup. We knew there would be no nice motels, restaurants or filling stations on the way, so we had to take the things we would need.

We had a special large wooden box for traveling. In it we packed the necessities for overnight stays. We expected to spend some nights at the bare government guest houses. This required taking along equipment for preparing meals, including a little portable kerosene stove, and canned and nonperishable food. For nights we would need bedding and mosquito nets for four beds. We packed personal clothing, plenty of drinking water, and our medicines. We were not likely to come across filling stations, so an additional supply of gas and oil must go too.

At last, all was packed in, the children readied, and we were off for Uganda. It was school vacation, so Joy and Happy (Len) could come with us.

Our way passed across the equator. It looked the same as the surrounding country, but it actually was the line between the northern and southern hemispheres. The crossing was marked by a monument, a huge cement "O" large enough for people to stand inside. We arranged ourselves in it and had a family picture taken. We had crossed the equator before, in the air and on the sea, but this was our first crossing on land.

We enjoyed our visit to the city of Kampala and also to the neighboring city, Entebbe. The Botanical Gardens in Entebbe were beautiful and amazing. We had a dip in the north end of Lake Victoria and there was also a lovely, clear swimming pool near Kampala. We had good family times there. Our house was near the mission church, so we met Christians from many missions and countries. An East Indian family invited us to their home and served us rice and curry. We liked it very much and learned to prepare this dish in our own home. They were very busy in the mission work and in leading their own people to Jesus.

It was decided that I needed some time alone, so arrangements were made for me to stay a few weeks at a lovely Ugandan resort, Kaptigut Arms. It was a beautiful and interesting place with many flowers and pleasant places to walk. There I saw monkeys hopping about in the trees. Also, there was a little stream and a waterfall to visit. The most amazing sight was the Rift Valley that runs from the Dead Sea in Israel way down to South Africa. I stood on the edge of the cliff and looked down into a broad valley. There were houses and cars and people there, but it seemed like another world. I had a restful time there and then my family came to get me. Vacation was nearly over; after a few more days in Kampala, we started the return journey.

As this was English territory, Leonard had to drive on the left. He did a good job until our last day. He started right, onto a roundabout, and was stopped by a police officer. He gave us only a warning when he understood that we came from a right-driving country.

All too soon we headed back to Congo. On our way we passed a famous game preserve, Park Albert, where elephants and other animals freely grazed not far from the road. It was early evening and we planned to spend the night at a lodge in the park. We could see the buildings in the distance when, all at once, something went wrong with our steering. We were in danger; no one could walk to the lodge to get help for fear of the animals. We did not like the idea of staying there all night.

I told Len to watch on one side and Joy on the other, and I held a flashlight while Leonard crawled under the car. He managed to wire parts together well enough to get us to the lodge. It took most of the next day to fix the car. While waiting, we watched hippos come down to the river to swim and find food; one passed very near Gay and me. This trip held many adventures for us.

We spent a few days at a mission in the Ruwensori Mountains (Mountains of the Moon). It was almost on the equator and situated at the foot of a glacier. A channel had been constructed to direct the melting ice water right into the mission compound. Every morning I dashed out to the back veranda and splashed icy water on my face. That was surely a good "waker-upper"! Brrrrr!

Then we were home again. Joy and Len were back in school and the four of us were left at Ikozi. A few months later, we were transferred to Katanti for the rest of that term.

CHAPTER EIGHT

SECOND TERM
REALLY BEGINS

The work of the mission was progressing. More families were stationed at Katanti, so homes were being built. Church and evangelistic activities were doing well, and medical work was increasing. Plans were being made to start a Bible School to train young men, and the Balega school was growing and also the school for missionary children, Berean Academy. As more families came, there were, of course, more children needing school. A few of the older kids were in high school. Our teachers, Bob and Helen Hendry, were doing a wonderful job.

Most of the school children lived full-time at Katanti, but a number came from our other mission stations and even some from other mission groups. These boarded at Katanti in the large brick house that Albert Jansen had built. This seemed to make a good dormitory. We were happy that our own children could live with us this time.

Everyone on the station cooperated with this school and tried to do things that would make a well-rounded program for these children. School should not be only classes and studies, but also learning to live with others and having good times with them. For the school children and all of us, we had a party each Friday evening. All the station families took turns planning the entertainment and providing refreshments. We also had soccer games, tennis, strolls in the jungle, and special activities. We had music classes and many of the students played accordions. The children playing these instruments helped with the church services for Balega and missionaries together.

One year we had two students in the last year of high school and Leonard and I were their class sponsors. We planned a great Sneak Day for those two and the one junior as there would be no one to celebrate with her the next year. We informed only the parents, readied the car, and packed a picnic lunch the evening before. Next morning very early we were ready. I pinned a note on Len's mosquito net, informing him of our plans and telling him that he was responsible for his two little sisters. We even pushed the car down to the road for fear the motor would wake people; then we were off to Shabunda.

A small swimming pool had been constructed in the little town. We had a great time swimming, visiting our friends there, checking out the "shopping mall" which was one small store, and enjoying the lunch. It was late afternoon before we returned home, tired but happy. Everyone had been surprised but survived very well without us.

My part was the medical work. I was training a few young men to be medical workers. They could then do the hands-on jobs. Our maternity work was not huge but growing. I trained some women to help with maternity and baby care work. We held weekly clinics for pregnant mothers and small children. Our dispensary was equipped with an old-fashioned wood cook stove. Here we could boil water and sterilize metal instruments, syringes and needles. I treated things that needed to be dry in the large pressure cooker in my kitchen. I could dry damp packages in the oven.

We treated wounds, sores, ulcers, malaria and other fevers, intestinal parasites, and even leprosy. A few times the wound or fever was so bad I had to send the patients to the hospital in Shabunda. I mixed many of our medicines such as salves, liniment, potions and cough syrup. I had a recipe book for meds just like a recipe book for cooking. I did a lot of this mixing at home on our veranda and used a wooden packing box for a table. One afternoon I was working there and saw a snake taking a nap between my box and the wall. I yelled "Nzoka" and immediately men came with large knives and finished him.

In my spare time I made dresses for our growing girls, underwear and pants for Leonard and Happy, and altered donated clothes. I also made curtains and bedspreads. I used a treadle sewing machine because the price of gasoline was too high to use the generator for sewing.

Another experience that stands out in my mind is the time we had to take a patient to the hospital in Shabunda. All our missionaries were at Katanti. The men were planning a trip way north of us to perhaps start a new work in that area. This would leave all the women to cope with the work at Katanti. We wondered what we would do in case of emergency. We would have a car but most did not know to drive. One other woman and I had done some driving but were badly out of practice. One of the men took us for a refresher course and then the men left.

Sure enough, an emergency occurred. One of the Balega young men was clearing forest to make a garden when the tree he was chopping fell on his leg and broke it. Setting broken bones was beyond my experience, so we had to take him to a doctor. Maxine and I started out, being quite nervous about our ability to make this trip. We were doing fine until we were nearly to Shabunda and had to cross the river on a primitive ferry. Maxine insisted that I drive on and off the ferry. It was very tricky to keep from driving right into the river. The Lord really helped us to arrive safely at our destination.

We took our patient to the hospital where he would be cared for. He was sure he was going to die. Probably before medical care was available, people did die when a fracture occurred. We assured him that the doctor would know what to do and that he would soon be well and strong again. We prayed with him and then left on our way home again. Isn't it strange? I vividly remember the trip to Shabunda but not a thing about the return trip. I guess it was sheer relief.

We survived that trip all right, but we had other interesting experiences when traveling. We did not travel much; gasoline was expensive and work was always pressing. We might make it to the city once or twice a year or visit another of our stations. Three instances of trouble on the road were caused by insects.

When one of our babies was just a few weeks old, we had been on a trip and were only a few miles from Katanti. When the car was climbing up a hill, the engine suddenly stopped. While the men worked to fix the trouble, the older children ran about and I sat in the car holding the baby. It was then early evening, the time when the mosquitoes came out in great numbers. We were all bitten but did not think much about it; it was the usual thing. About a day later, the baby became very ill. We took her to the doctor in Shabunda where he treated her for severe malaria. She soon recovered and had no more trouble.

Once we were making a trip in our Studebaker pickup. As we rounded a hilly curve, a back wheel fell into a large hole in the road. We found the cause; the road had been undergirded with forest poles. Termites had gotten into the wood and eaten away so much of it that the weight of our car had broken through.

Another insect episode occurred when the motor stopped while we were traveling. While the men worked on the car, the children and I found a comfortable seat along an embankment. When I stood up later, a Mulega came by and scrutinized the place. He scratched away a little dirt and there was a live scorpion. I had been sitting on a scorpion's nest! It was God who kept me from being bitten. Though scorpion bites are usually not fatal, they are very painful.

Once while traveling from Katanti to Ikozi we ran into a very strong rainstorm. In the pickup with us was a man recovering from a serious wound and a pregnant woman just about ready to deliver. As we topped a mountain pass, it began to rain very hard. It was so much rain that the hill above began sliding down into the road and the roadway was slipping down into the valley. We were caught between two landslides! We were near a government post where a jail was also located. The children and I slugged through the mud to the commander. He allowed the prisoners to come and dig our car out of the landslide.

We are all on a journey through life. Many times we encounter dangers. Sometimes we don't even realize the danger, but the Lord knows and cares for all who trust in Him.

LANGUAGE PROGRESS

All along we were learning new Kilega words and trying to improve our ability to speak it. One day the cattle drivers from Rwanda came by. Usually we could not buy a whole cow because we could not take care of so much meat. This time there were enough families living on the station that we could take a whole animal. When we butchered this cow, I grabbed a notebook and pen and ran to watch the doings. It was my chance to learn the Kilega words for the inner organs of the body. After that, I put together a medical dictionary in English, Kilega and French. It was quite a help to me and other medical workers.

Our first language incident occurred just a few days after our arrival. Happy, not yet four, had been playing with an African boy and came back saying, "Kasamena says, 'Hapana.'" That means "No." Happy was off to a good start. Often children learn faster than adults.

Back in Leonard's early days, he had experienced a little language difficulty. A car was stuck in the mud and he had a crew of workers ready to push it out. He carefully stationed them in places and said to them, "Dendila!" He expected them to push but nothing happened. He tried it again; no result. Finally, someone caught on and told him that the word he needed was "Sindika" (push). He had been telling them to "Dendila" which meant "Wait."

Kilega is an interesting language and not too difficult to learn because there are few exceptions to the rules. It is confusing at first because there are nine different categories for nouns, each of which has certain prefixes for singular and plural. One group is only about people, another is for things, another for animals, and so forth. For instance, a noun referring to a person starts with the prefix "mu" ("mutu," a person), while the noun referring to people starts with "ba" ("bantu"). One thing is "kintu" and many "bintu." Animals start with "n" ("nyama"), both singular and plural. Any adjectives must agree with the noun form as "muntu mulazi" would be a tall person. There were consonant combinations, as with "m" the combinations were "mb" and "mp." With "n," they used "ng," "nk," "ns," "nt," "ny." Verbs were complex. With prefixes and suffixes, a verb could be built up as a person spoke, perhaps telling an entire story in one word.

I was not particularly good at the language; those better at this art began trying to translate Gospel songs and parts of the Bible. About that time a teacher named Lauback came to all the different missions in the area. He said that translating the Bible was fine, but what good would it do unless the people knew how to read? Then he gave us some good ideas for teaching the people.

I was very interested in this project. I was astonished to find that our brightest primary students were not learning to read. Why not? The ancient way of teaching was simply for the teacher to recite or read the subject matter. Then the pupils repeated it after the teacher. This would be repeated until they knew it well. After all, in their grandparents' day, they had no paper, no pens, no blackboards or books. What other way did they have to teach? Thus, the brightest ones soon memorized the lesson, but they were not learning what those little marks on the page were trying to tell them. We decided to remedy this situation. I began to compose a very simple Kilega primer. First were two letters and their sounds, "a" and "b." Next day we added another letter, "n." That made it possible for the students to put the letters together to make the work "bana," meaning children. Each day they learned a new letter and soon knew enough letters to read simple stories about family and usual daily events.

Our oldest, Joy, was about twelve then. We selected a few of the smartest school girls to come for special lessons. They gathered on our veranda and Joy taught the lesson. With this new approach, they learned rapidly and soon were leaders among the women and children. I eventually worked out a series of three readers. By the third reader, students could read Bible stories. One of the missionary children was quite an artist. She drew illustrations for the stories. Then about that time, a new missionary arrived with an early form of a Xerox machine. He was able to print these little books. Not too long ago I was informed that they are still using my books to teach Balega children to read. I was delighted to think I had done something of lasting importance.

Near the end of this term, another child was added to our family, another girl, making us a family of seven. We named her Melodie to continue our tradition of cheerful names: Joy, Happy (Leonard Leigh), Merry Sue, Gay, and now Melodie. For her birth we went to a guest house of a mining company fairly close to Ikozi. The company doctor had agreed to help with the birth. We went about a week early and stayed in a mud-walled, metal-roofed guest house until time. I often joke that we first came to Congo with two children, went home with three, returned with four and finally went home with five. I had always wanted a sizable family and Leonard had insisted that he wanted a little daughter. He might later have regretted that statement, but here he was with four girls and he loved every one.

It was a busy term with much progress being made. The children were learning and growing. Of course, there were trials and difficulties but also much joy and satisfaction. These years at Katanti were about the happiest and most productive of all three terms.

CHAPTER NINE
SECOND TRIP HOME

It seemed very soon, but it was now time for our second furlough. We started our trip home with an auto drive north from Katanti to the Uku area. We stayed there overnight and found the climate much damper than ours.

Next morning we went to the jungle airstrip to wait for the small inland plane. When we knew the plane was near, all the men started chasing baboons off the landing field. On the flight to Stanleyville, we encountered a strong rainstorm but landed safely at the international airport.

When the next plane was ready, we were ushered on board first because we now had four older children and Baby Melodie. The

Belgians liked families and gave them special privileges. To our surprise, the plane was air-conditioned which made it very comfortable.

Our first stop was at Khartoum, Sudan. We all went into the airport to wait while the plane was refueled. When we went back to the plane for takeoff, we were just getting settled when we were told to get off and go back to the airport. A fierce sandstorm had blown up and flying was not safe, so we waited out the storm and then took off for Cairo.

There the plane was refueled again and started out over the Mediterranean. We had not gone far when one of the propeller engines failed, perhaps damaged by the sandstorm. There was nothing to do but return to Cairo and wait for another engine to be flown in. Meanwhile, we were furnished a nice hotel room, a lunch, and then a trip across the Nile to visit the pyramids and the Sphinx.

It was like a dream come true to actually be there and see the marvels. I had studied about these pyramids years before but never imagined that I would be right there. Then we were taken to the wonderful Egyptian museum. We saw images of pharaohs, precious jewelry, and ancient artifacts. We also visited a perfume factory. Because we were Americans and Europeans, the Egyptians thought we had a lot of money and would buy much of their fine extracts. We could not fulfill their expectations. We were inconvenienced by this interruption but it made a wonderful adventure possible. The one bad thing was that we were terribly thirsty. I had taken water along but it was gone before we reached the pyramids. Later, they offered us Coke, but what we wanted was water.

Finally, the plane was readied and we resumed our journey to Brussels. On landing there, we had a second experience of a tire blowing out. Our pilot skillfully made a safe landing, but it was scary. We visited a dear Belgian friend and the next day we took off for London. We flew across the English Channel in a speedy, new type of plane, landing at London's famous airport, Heathrow.

While in London, we were able to see Westminster Abby, Buckingham Palace, Big Ben, and the Thames; however, we planned this trip especially to visit Stoneleigh Abbey. This was another amazing experience, especially for me. My name is Hazel Leigh. My paternal grandmother often told me about our English heritage through the Leigh family of Warwickshire. The Leigh tradition goes back to Queen Elizabeth I. Thomas Leigh was knighted and served as Lord Mayor of London. There were many famous Leighs after that and the family owned a wonderful estate, Stoneleigh Abbey, our ancestral home. It was a lovely mansion with many valuable family paintings, carvings and furnishings. We were shown the suite that Queen Victoria and her husband occupied on a visit there. The private breakfast room had been redecorated with hand-painted wallpaper. Jane Austen and her mother also visited there; Jane's mother, Cassandra, was of the Leigh family. After a memorable afternoon tour, we returned to London and spent the night at a bed and breakfast accommodation.

The next morning we took off from London, stopped at Birmingham, and then across the Atlantic, landing at New York and then Detroit. Friends from DBI lived there and invited us to stay with them a few days. They also helped us find a car, a Ford station wagon, which suited our needs. We made Joy and Len comfortable in the back, Merry Sue could sleep on the back seat, Gay had a special tiny bed just back of the front seat, and I could hold Baby Melodie. We were all set for furlough transportation. We used that car all through our furlough and then sold it for what we had paid; it was a good vehicle.

After a week or so in Detroit, we started out to visit friends and relatives in Colorado and Nebraska. Our home church in North Platte arranged for a house and we settled down there for several months.

We did some traveling, but not so much as the first furlough. Four children were in school. We needed to stay put so they could keep up their proper grades. Joy and Len were in high school and the others in elementary. Leonard was working for the mission and was away from home many times. He was also trying to raise more support for us. Some of our faithful supporters had died or were unable to continue and now we had another child.

We had to adapt our lifestyle to living in the USA. For one thing, I had to care for our home, do the cooking, laundry, ironing and cleaning. I was spoiled by having Balega house helpers in Congo, but I did not have all the other tasks here that I had had in the Congo.

I really enjoyed being an ordinary housewife and caring for the children. It was good to go to church and speak and hear English and to take part in various activities. Our pastor kept us busy, giving us tasks to do for the church.

We spent some time in Colorado Springs because we were offered housing there. The winter was very cold, snow was deep, and icicles reached from the roof to the ground. As Congo never gets snow, we thought at first it was a great experience, but we soon got tired of the cold and inconvenience. Melodie was about eighteen months then. We were amused when she called the snow "nony."

After a few months in Colorado Springs, we moved back to North Platte and stayed there until time to return to the work in Congo.

CHAPTER TEN

THIRD TERM BEGINS

O ur third term started with a very difficult decision. Joy was ready for her last year of high school. What kind of college education could she get in Congo? Perhaps she could take correspondence instruction? Some dear friends from Bible school days suggested that we leave her with them. They were working with the Back to the Bible Broadcast in Lincoln, Nebraska. They already had twin sons finishing high school and a younger daughter. Why should they want to take on another responsibility? After much prayer, we decided that this would be the best course for Joy and she agreed. So our trip began with a very sad farewell. Happy, our son, was a year behind Joy so we took him with us; we would consider his needs when necessary.

Our first flight to Africa had taken three days and nights; this one went much more smoothly. We left New York City Thursday afternoon and arrived at Katanti Station Saturday afternoon, the fastest trip ever. On our way, we were to stop in Brussels, Belgium, to change planes. We arrived at Brussels, but the airstrip was fogged in. We circled the city for about an hour while we used up the remaining fuel, thus making landing safer. When the plane descended, we found that the last few feet were clear so we landed safely.

Now we were behind schedule. Thankfully, our plane for Africa was held up for us and we were hurriedly escorted to the waiting plane. Landing in Stanleyville, we quickly shed our winter clothes and soon boarded a small Congolese plane headed for Bukavu. We refueled at a small landing strip fairly close to our area. Leonard found a Congolese who owned a car and he agreed to transport us to Katanti. This saved other missionaries the long trip to Bukavu to get us. In about three hours we were at Katanti!

If we thought we had had adventures before, this term held many unusual experiences for us. This third term lasted four years and during that time we lived in four different areas among four tribes and four languages. We lived in ten different dwellings and did four types of work. It makes me dizzy to even remember. This eventful term, however, began and ended at our special home station, Katanti.

First, there was not an empty house for us, so for a time we five lived with a large family, plus a second family of four and the five of us, all in the same house. Then we had a room in our permanent cement-block Bible school building while school was not in session. We didn't have a kitchen so we cooked and ate in an old native-style house that was falling apart. It was adequate for a short time. Later, someone went on furlough and we moved into our dear first Katanti home once more.

The missionary children's school was going fine. Some students from other stations and other missions attended and they boarded with Katanti families. There were many activities for the children and they all seemed to be doing fine. Merry Sue and Gay attended the station school. Melodie was still quite young.

A Bible school for Balega men had been started. The cement-block building had been built for it. Everyone had their jobs to do and cooperated, so the work was going forward. Church services were well attended by the villagers and even our local witch doctor came. Some missionary children and adults played musical instruments, mostly accordions, and this helped a lot with the church services. The Balega loved to sing various hymns and gospel songs that had been translated into Kilega. Some of the Balega Christian elders took turns with the missionary men in giving the messages from the Bible.

We were all busy and happy, but Congo was due to obtain independence from Belgium in the spring of 1961. What would that mean for us? Very few Congolese had been trained in government, management, economics or politics. Most had no idea what independence might mean. Many thought it would mean freedom from white men and great riches for each one of them. They were not trained to carry on their own government. For awhile after the set date, all seemed to be okay, but after a period of time some Congolese men began asserting their authority.

They demanded that all white men turn in their guns so they would be unable to fight back. They made other regulations, put up road blocks, wanted to know all our business and where we were going. Because we could speak their language, they didn't cause us much trouble except the inconvenience. Things, however, were getting more serious. Most of the Belgians had left, and native Congolese were determined to show us who was in charge. Finally, we decided it would be wise to leave for a time; we all needed a vacation anyway. We went to a delightful missions resort on Lake Kivu called Kumbia. We stayed a few weeks and then it seemed safe for us to return to our stations in the forest.

We wanted to keep in touch with our daughter Joy, but communications were disrupted. At that time, we could not even get our usual weekly mail. In the past, we had sent a runner on foot to the state post to bring the mail back to us. Now, however, it took as long as a month before news got through. We were at a remote location in the jungle and had no e-mail, computers, Skype, telephones, or newspapers. Shortwave radio was used only for business or emergencies.

UKU

We returned to our stations and tried to carry on all our usual ministries but it was never the same. There was tension in the air and we all wondered what would come next. After a time, it was decided that our family should move to our newest station, Uku, far north of Katanti. This station had been open only a year or so. The people, a tribe called Bakumu, were much like the Balega, but their language was a little different. We tried to begin ministries such as school, church, some medical work, and improved agriculture.

Though we loved our mud house at Katanti, this cement-block house was very nice. It was almost two houses. The main part was a kitchen and living and dining room with a floored attic for storage. The other part was bath and two bedrooms. A delightful breezeway had been constructed between the two parts. We had some Bakumu house helpers to cook and clean but we took care of the bedrooms ourselves.

Merry Sue had elected to come with us, but Gay stayed at Katanti for her schooling. Melodie was only about five so she was with us. This meant that I must home school the two girls. Merry Sue was in fifth grade and Melodie in first. With a little instruction, Merry Sue could go ahead on her own most of the time and Melodie did not need a lot of help. That meant that I had time for the medical work and other ministries.

A young single man, Carl Moyer, worked with us. He had had some dental training and could do simple dental work for our people which they greatly appreciated.

The work was more difficult there. Contrary to our Balega, these people did not so readily welcome missionaries or even Christian ministry from other Balega. We were learning more about them and their language differences. We were quite happy there and excited about future opportunities to proclaim the gospel; however, the political unrest was increasing. The men were trying to keep tabs on the situation as the news was passed along from person to person.

One afternoon a Mulega came with disturbing news. He had been talking with other Africans who told him that there was a serious disturbance up north, near Stanleyville. We were not too worried about this, but we learned much later that affairs for missionaries in that area were critical; some missionaries were killed in the uprising. Carl heard these rumors and felt that we ought to leave. "Well, okay," I said. "We can pack up this evening and leave early in the morning." But he insisted that we must leave that very afternoon. We did a hurried job of packing essentials, leaving many things behind. Little did we realize that what we packed in our suitcases and one small trunk would be our living materials for about two years. We never did return to that station, as it did not seem advisable to reopen the station in the midst of such troubles. Recently, we heard that Christian Balega are doing some work in that area.

It was at least a four-hour trip for us, Leonard and I, Merry Sue and Melodie. I think Carl had his own car and we had just bought an open van from missionaries who had had to leave. We also took some Balega helpers with us. Some were from the Katanti area and were glad to be going back home.

KATANTI

It was late in the evening when we arrived at Katanti. We found the missionaries there were also alarmed by the rumors they had heard. We all decided it would be best to leave. I remember thinking that we were all in danger and wondering what we could do. What if we were not permitted to leave? What about our children? The closest way to help was to the east. We all packed up and left very early the next morning, headed east to our other station, Ikozi. We spent that night there with our missionaries who also thought we should leave. This meant that all the Berean missionaries from all four or five stations were together there. It was amazing that the Ikozi people quickly found places for all to sleep and provided food for the whole group. So we were all together, praying and wondering what we should do. Our questions were answered early that very afternoon in a way that left no doubt. God had promised to direct our paths and He did.

IKOZI

The Congolese had earlier ordered all foreigners to turn in their guns. Suddenly, here came a group of angry natives, yelling and threatening us. They had gotten news that we still had a gun on the premises and they were indignant. Immediately, all the missionary men and our Balega leaders went out to meet them. We soon found out that their purpose was to get our guns or punish us. On further investigation, we learned that the gun in question was a BB gun that the teenagers had used to shoot at monkeys! What a lot of fuss over what was hardly more than a toy. Unfortunately, the teens had taken that BB gun out to the jungle and we had no way to reach them.

While the tension was high, we took all the children, especially the teen-aged girls, into the big rock house and guarded the doors. Ordinarily we trusted our Balega people, but these were not of our area and some of them seemed to be intoxicated. These visitors demanded that all our men come out and form a half circle before them. Then it really touched our hearts to see that every Balega elder had stationed himself before one of the missionaries. If these visitors wished to harm the white men, they would have to face the Balega first!

EVACUATION

When the kids returned with the gun and things had calmed down, our elders consulted with us. They said they knew that they were in for a difficult time; however, if we stayed, their first concern would be our safety. We realized that we would actually be an added burden to them, so we all figured it would be best to leave for a time. God had seen us through a very tense encounter. At the same time, He was directing us for our immediate future.

This incident had happened mid-morning and we decided to leave then. We packed our necessities and headed east. Some of us would never again see the possessions we were leaving behind. For others it would be months before they would regain the articles they had thought were necessary. For us, what we brought would be our supply for over a year for a family of five, including three growing girls. God took care of us and did supply our needs along the way.

BUKAVU

It was a full day's drive to Bukavu over narrow, twisting mountain roads. It was late evening when we pulled in to a Conservative Baptist Mission on a hill overlooking the city. The missionaries there kindly found places for all to sleep. We were a caravan of about six cars and twenty-nine people; nearly half were children. The next morning we went into Bukavu to see if we could get permission to leave Congo. On the way into town we came to a road block and one of our vehicles, a new pickup, was nearly confiscated. The Congolese who was going to drive, however, was unable to start the motor so he gave the truck back to us.

Things were very tense there. Because of the unsettled conditions, the United Nations had set up headquarters in Bukavu. They had placed a contingent of soldiers on one of the peninsulas jutting out into Lake Kivu. We asked for their help in our situation and they directed us to wait there for awhile. They found places for us to spend the night in empty houses the Belgians had vacated. I remember that we could not find a place for five-year-old Melodie, so we made a bed for her on a wide closet shelf.

UNITED NATIONS HEADQUARTERS IN BUKAVU

Next morning we were anxiously waiting for news but nothing was happening. I had an opportunity to buy a bunch of fresh vegetables and decided to cook up a stew while we were waiting. The stew was bubbling merrily on a portable kerosene stove in the middle of the bare front room floor. Then the news came that we were leaving immediately. I doused the fire, put a lid on the pot, gathered up my family, and we were ready to move. Our caravan was headed for the Ruzizi, the small river that marks the border between Congo and Rwanda. There was a guardhouse at the border and we had to present our sheaf of permits, one for each family.

Suddenly, the Congolese guards began shouting at us, all excited and angry. They telephoned headquarters downtown and yelled in authoritative voices. We were wondering what was wrong and were somewhat frightened and especially concerned about the children. The guard said that we did not have permission to cross the river, so they decided to take us all in to headquarters. They positioned an armed guard in each of our cars and took us to the Congolese authorities. What would they do to us? Put us in jail? Kill us? It really was quite frightening. We tried to shield the children from danger.

Our guard was a Mulega who was surprised that we could speak Kilega. That made a good impression. We were escorted to the office where our men met with the commander. In a short time we were permitted to leave. What had happened was that each family had a permission form, but the one in charge had signed only the top one, expecting that it would be sufficient for the whole group. The border guards were not satisfied with that. The commander then signed all the other permits and we were free! Another very tense moment successfully endured. It was not really such a big affair and easily remedied, but to us who experienced it, it seemed very frightening.

So we all crossed the river safely though a little shook up. People on the Rwanda side had been watching and sympathizing with us. The Red Cross people met and comforted us. They offered the children packets of dry Jell-O and the children ate it like candy. I had never thought of doing that, but the kids enjoyed it.

We were all grateful to those people and especially to our Lord. We formed a circle of prayer and thanksgiving and sang the well-known hymn, "Amazing Grace."

"Through many dangers, toils and snares, we have already come; 'Tis Grace that led us safe thus far, and Grace will lead us home."

Never was that song so true for us! Then we were hungry and shared that pot of stew that I had made and brought along through all this.

Although this was already late afternoon, we proceeded south along the Ruzizi River to Bujumbura, the capital of Burundi. Here American officials met us and wanted to know all that had happened. Somehow we all found places to spend the night, mostly at nearby mission stations. The next day each family had to decide what to do next. Our group split up, some returning to the USA and one group going to work with an English mission in Tanzania. We decided to stay in the area for a time. We had not been back in Congo very long and were not ready to return home so soon.

CHAPTER ELEVEN

LIFE AS REFUGEES

BUJUMBURA, BURUNDI

Since we were officially refugees, we were offered a place in a displaced persons camp in Bujumbura which had been set up in the school for children of East Indian parentage. This was vacation time for the students so we occupied the classrooms. Meals were catered from a nearby hotel at a reasonable price. At first, our family was granted a classroom by ourselves, but more refugees were arriving almost daily. Consequently, two dorms were set up, one for men and boys, and one for women and children. We were given two beds for the four of us. Keeping clothes clean was a problem. We took turns using the equipment which consisted of a small tub and a single, coldwater faucet. We hung the washed clothes on the bushes to dry. There was not much to do but wait; we had time to read, sew and walk about.

After about two weeks of this, one of the missions in the city heard about the missionaries staying in the refugee camp and expressed concern for us. A Scandinavian mission offered us a place to stay for a time. We moved to this more compatible place, a large guest room where we could all be together. We were very grateful to these people. I especially remember tea times, "quatre heure," hot tea and cookies served each afternoon on the veranda.

It was while we were there that an earthquake occurred. It was quite a strong quake and aftershocks lasted off and on most of the day. Perhaps these were shocks from the volcano at the north end of Lake Kivu about 200 miles north of Bujumbura. Store windows were shattered and tiles shaken from walls. People in apartment buildings moved out to the park for the day, lest the buildings fall down about them. Leonard and I searched for a better vehicle. We found one we liked, but there was no key with which to lock it. Because of such troublous times, we did not like this idea.

We had left the girls at our room and the missionary there had assured us she would look out for them. The cook had put some food in a pressure cooker and turned on the gas. The gas and electricity went off because of the quake and no cooking was going on. After a time, however, the gas came back on without warning. The cooker began to heat and the pressure built up until the cooker "blew its top." I think the lid hit the ceiling; no one had thought to check on the gas situation.

Meanwhile, our friends in Rwanda at the Free Methodist Mission, Kibagora, were doing quite well. They were building the first permanent church for the station and were nearly ready to put on the roof. They surely could use more help in directing the work. They suggested that Leonard and I serve there for awhile. Also, there was a mission school at Mweya in Burundi where Merry Sue and Ruth Gay could continue their education. Melodie who was five was still too young for school, but Len was missing school. Friends in St. Louis had offered to keep any of the missionary young people if anyone wished to send a child home to the USA. That seemed best for Len. He flew back to St. Louis to stay with Olive and Glen Lindquist for his last year of high school.

KIBAGORA, RWANDA

So we told Len good-by and left the girls and returned north to Kibagora. Though the language was different, we managed quite well. Leonard worked on the construction and I was able to help at the hospital. They furnished a small apartment for us and a native cook/ servant to help. I also was teaching Melodie simple first-grade subjects, Bible stories and verses. We stayed there several months and were quite happy except that our two daughters were so far away.

The girls were well cared for. The teacher there, Katherine Hendricks, and the dorm parents, the Millers, were very helpful. The Millers had a small daughter, Ruth, about Melodie's age and two boys. Strangely enough, I was to meet that little girl again, all grown up and a grand-mother. I also met her parents and the teacher in the USA many years later.

MUYEBE AND MWEYA

When we were no longer needed at Kibagora, we were offered a position at a Free Methodist station at Muyebe, Burundi. Missionaries there were to return home and a couple was badly needed at that sta-tion. This seemed a solution for us and we were happy to move there, especially as it was only a half-hour drive to the school at Mweya. The missionaries who were leaving stayed several days and helped us learn our way around. We lived in their guest house for awhile though there was no electricity or running water. There was an outhouse and for baths we went to the main house. When they left, we moved into the main house which had three bedrooms, living room, an office, storage room, bath and kitchen, more than adequate for the three of us and still plenty of room. The two older girls, Merry Sue and Ruth Gay, were at school most of the time. Sometimes the girls could spend a weekend with us; it was so good to have them near. Several times we spent a weekend at the school.

We were quite happy there for about a year. Leonard supervised the whole station and I helped at the dispensary some, but the Burundi "infirmiers" were doing quite well. I spent most of my time teaching in the school for Burundi girls. They were considerably more advanced than our girls in Congo who were just now being allowed to attend primary school. Most of these Burundi girls had learned some French and had received quite a bit of education. Now they were being trained to be teachers for their own people.

I taught a hygiene class but mostly taught sewing and other handcrafts. One of our projects required that each girl design and make her own dress. Not only this, but she was required to make her own pattern for the dress. The mission bought a bolt of material and each girl produced a nice dress. The dresses were all of the same material, but each chose her own collar and sleeve treatment. I was very proud of them.

Of course there was the language problem. Even in the neighboring countries, Rwanda and Burundi, there was considerable difference. There were similarities, however, between Kilega and Kirundi that really helped. Sometimes I taught in French; sometimes another missionary translated for us. I remember that in both languages "landa" meant "sew" and "landula" meant "unsew" or "rip it out." I'm sure they hated that word.

We had a maid to help with the housework and be with Melodie when I was out. She was a Burundi girl named Kasikazia; we just called her Kassi. She was a good helper. Our Balega girls were not permitted to work for missionaries, being too valuable for the work at home and incapable of book learning, or so the men thought.

We had some good times with the students at Mweya. Sometimes we could visit for a day or two. One weekend we took over the work of the dorm and let the regular dorm parents take some time off. That was a good experience for all of us. Much later, the dorm parents told us how much that break had meant to them for they were about stressed out. Another time we invited the entire school to spend the weekend with us. We had a glorified slumber party, a picnic and treasure hunt, games, and lots of fun. As I look back, I wonder how we managed the large meals and beds for everyone, but we did and everyone, even Leonard and I, had a grand time.

Another incident happened about that time. Food was scarce because the rains were so abundant that people could not get into their fields to plant. Humanitarian agencies sent in staple food. One of Leonard's jobs was to distribute supplies to people according to a specified order. Once a man thought he was not getting his fair share and began an angry protest. Other dissatisfied persons joined in and the affair became dangerous, especially for Leonard. Not knowing the language, he could not understand the trouble or do anything about it. He locked himself in the office and sent out some of the Christian men for help. There was an old pickup handy, so I grabbed the keys and Melodie and drove to the nearest Free Methodist station. It was manned by the son of the Adamsons with whom we had served in Rwanda. I was in such a hurry I didn't check for water in the radiator, so it was steaming when we got there. The missionary came quickly, ferreted out the problem and managed to quiet the mob. Again, it showed how easily a fairly simple situation could explode into real trouble.

While we were at Muyebe, others of our mission were working at an English mission in Tanzania. We managed to visit them and hold a mission conference. They were sending their children to school at Rift Valley Academy near Nairobi. A nice feature of that trip was to visit the Serengeti Game Reserve. We saw lions, antelope, hippos, ostriches, giraffes and other wildlife in their natural habitat.

About that time, Leonard began having painful digestive trouble. The local doctor sent him to Nairobi for examination. It was discovered that he was allergic to beef. All he had to do was avoid eating beef. We were careful for years after that, but he finally overcame it. I also experienced the trip to Nairobi. We returned to the other missionaries by a lovely boat trip on Lake Victoria.

I had heard a European woman remark that Congo had had the sickness, but now was on the mend, whereas Rwanda and Burundi were now catching the fever. Trouble was brewing. We heard that there was now comparative calm in our home area so, perhaps, it would be safe to return to our jungle. We packed up and left Muyebe. We drove around the north end of Lake Tanganyika and a little way south to visit a Free Methodist mission on that side. The lake water had so increased that water was nearly over the lakeside road in places. For awhile, we drove north with the left wheel on land and the right in the water. Finally, we arrived back at Bukavu. All our missionaries had planned to meet there and decide what to do.

CYANGUGU, RWANDA

Just opposite Bukavu on the Rwanda side was a sister city, Cyangugu. A mission there gave us the use of a large house for a time, and five or six families gathered there. It was decided to send our men into our area to scout out the situation. We were a bit afraid to send them but, after prayer, we felt that was the thing to do. We women and children waited anxiously for news. After a week or so, the men returned with good news and we all prepared to return to our stations in the forest.

CHAPTER TWELVE
RETURN TO KATANTI

We felt it would be best to all stay together for a while. As Ikozi was not adequate for all of us, we went to our next station, Katchungu. This had been a Belgian state post with three good houses and office buildings. We had had our own doctor for a term and he had advanced the building of a permanent brick hospital. Our family was allotted part of the hospital building for a temporary home. The building had a wood cook stove, originally for the hospital but adequate for our use. Again, we had no electricity or running water.

Our Balega leaders had a sad tale for us. Rebel forces had overrun all our stations, destroying property and tearing up books and documents. They had poured our precious medicines and chemicals down the drain. One incident was told of a rebel grabbing bottles of agents that he knew nothing about and pouring out the contents. These bottles contained dangerous chemicals and released bad fumes, and he was overcome. On each station most of our books were torn apart and some valuable papers of translation work, English to Kilega, were destroyed. It seemed the rebels wanted to defeat anyone with education and a better style of living.

When our people knew the enemy forces were approaching, they had disappeared into the jungle. Balega leaders and more educated Congolese had hid out with them. We had left our radio and they were able to follow the progress of the rebel forces. They always felt they were in danger, staying a day or a month in one place. When they could, they built simple dwellings of sticks, vines and leaves.

One day they were fleeing and came to a large river. There were no boats there for the crossing. Usually a few boats were tied up at the trail crossings, but the enemy had been there and cut all the boats loose to foil any opposition. The river was too swift to swim and there were crocodiles in these waters. The rebels had loosed the boats there and then gone upstream to cut more boats loose at the next crossing. These boats floated downstream just in time to save God's people. This was surely a case of our enemies falling into their own trap.

Our Balega people were very happy to have the missionaries back and we were happy to be home again after such a long time. We all hoped to restart programs that had been interrupted for over a year. Everyone had a job in the work. The school for our children was resumed at Katchungu. The two excellent teachers, Helen and Bob Hendry, were ready to teach classes for about ten students in different grades. Some medical work was begun with Balega assistants doing most of the work now. I explored the storage rooms in the hospital attic and found a set of optometrist's lenses. There was also a textbook on the subject. I studied and then began to test the eyes of some of the Balega who knew how to read but had poor eyesight.

I could order glasses from Bukavu. I certainly did not have the training of a professional ophthalmologist. I must have done something right, for my patients were delighted with the improvement the glasses made in their sight. There were sometimes delays, however, because a shipment of frames had been stolen. This was caused by their idea that people who wore glasses were more intelligent. They thought that even wearing the empty frames would give them wisdom!

Soon I got invitations from neighboring missions to come and test their scholars for glasses. I enjoyed this work, especially when I saw the gratitude they felt at being able to see better. I went to at least two other missions, stayed a week or so, and checked eyes for their people; several did need glasses. Also, I tried to teach the older boys how glasses work. The curvature of the glass bends the light rays so they focus on the right spot in the back of the eye. The problem was getting the right curvature for each eye. They had some queer ideas; for instance, one fellow who already had glasses came, saying, "Mama, these glasses have used up the medicine. Please put some more medicine in them."

KATANTI

After a time together at Katchungu, we were able to reopen the two older stations, Ikozi and Katanti, and we were sent to Katanti. That meant we had to leave Merry Sue and Ruth Gay at Katchungu for school. The families stationed there accepted the duty of boarding students from the other stations even though space was limited. We missed our girls, but I now had the task of teaching Melodie first grade.

They say that one difficulty with homeschooling is that the kids have trouble realizing the difference between mom (or dad) as the parent and then as the teacher. Melodie solved this difficulty herself. After breakfast she would say, "Good-bye, Mom, I have to go to school now." She would walk down the road a ways, then return saying,

"Good morning, Teacher. I'm ready for school." We had a pleasant schoolroom upstairs in the brick house by a window overlooking the slope down to the narrow, grass-grown "highway," our tenuous link with the outside world. We didn't have appropriate primers for her or teacher's manuals for me, but we made good progress. I had already taught the two older children and some others, so I knew about what we needed to cover. For one thing, we read all the way through *The Little Golden Illustrated Dictionary*. We found it interesting and it added to her vocabulary. We added art, poetry and songs to keep school interesting. We really had a lot of fun.

During this time I was often busy with the medical work. By now, the trained Balega fellows could do the ordinary work, and the trained women midwives could manage most deliveries. I mostly helped by compounding medicines and ointments and sterilizing instruments and dressing packages in our large pressure cooker.

Once we had a quite premature baby girl. She was so small that I padded a shoebox for her. This we kept in our pantry because the brick chimney from the cook stove ran through it and kept the baby warm. The mother slept on the pantry floor to be near her child. The baby could not nurse well so I found a tiny baby bottle among the girls' toys and this worked well. She gained weight and soon could be cared for as usual. She grew up to be a fine healthy little girl.

We were able to help another little girl. As we stopped at a village one day, I noticed a child with only one leg. She was trying to hop around but not doing very well. I got permission to take her to the mission for help. I hoped her parents were not expecting that we could give her back her leg. We could not do that, but we could help. I had the carpenters carve out a pair of crutches; I padded the arm rests well and had her try them for length. Then our fellows taught her how to use them. She was delighted that she could now walk upright and by herself. It was amazing to think what a difference those two sticks of wood made in her life. I hoped that someone would make her new crutches if these wore out and that longer crutches would be available as she grew taller.

On our return to Katanti, Leonard and I started a new ministry. We already had elementary school for the children and Bible school for older students. We were depending on them to teach the people in the villages, but we wanted to reach more of the ordinary people. We devised a very simple study of the main basic doctrines of the Bible and trained our helpers. Then we selected a central village and invited all those in that area to meet there one evening a week for this study. The course included key verses for them to memorize.

The people came from all around and were very interested. We kept attendance and memory verse records. When they finished the course of eight or ten lessons, each person was given a handmade certificate. The people greatly appreciated these, showing that they had accomplished something good.

We did this at different localities three or four times. This proved to help the people become grounded in God's Word. This was a trend in missions called TEE, Theological Training by Extension, or going out to the people. We did not know that this was being done, but we saw the need and tried to meet it.

About this time, a sort of cult spread over our area. Some of it was good and some quite radical. The members tried to infiltrate our area, but our trained villagers saw their error and resisted the cult. This made us feel that our work had been useful and blessed.

Though it was nearing the end of our term, we tried another new thing. Remember that this was back in the early sixties. Most of the eastern missions were operating on the colonial system. On these mission stations the Europeans lived at one end and there was a village of Congolese at the other end. In many fields the missionaries came in and lived right with the natives, but we did not. Though the Balega knew that we came to help them and give them the Word of God, there was not that close fellowship there ought to have been. So, once a week, we invited one Balega family to come and eat dinner with us. We enjoyed this very much and we hoped they did too.

By this time we had been on the field more than four years. We had worked in four areas with four different languages and people of four different tribes. We had lived in seven houses, and done four different kinds of work. Now we were growing weary. Though a term was usually five years, we asked to cut this one several months short. Our big reason was to be in the USA in time for Joy's graduation from nurse's training in Omaha, Nebraska. So we began packing, giving away and selling our possessions and preparing for our trip home. Melodie was about eight; Gay and Merry Sue were teenagers.

CHAPTER THIRTEEN
THIRD TRIP HOME

At last, this very eventful term was over. We finished just where we had begun, Katanti. As we drove down our mission road to the "highway," I had mixed emotions. Perhaps I was relieved to be out of the turmoil and uncertainty, but I was sad to be leaving, for an indefinite period, our Balega friends and fellow workers to face dangers ahead. Our family for this trip consisted of two adults and three girls, Merry Sue, Gay and Melodie.

A fellow worker drove us to Bakavu. Since there was always business and shopping to be done there, the trip could have two purposes. After the long, tiring trip to the city, we spent the night at a mission near Bakavu. The next morning we made our way to the airstrip. For some reason we were a bit rushed but, as we were leaving the country, we were required to go through customs. One important reason for this was to be sure we were not exporting ivory. As the Congo government had not set up a proper customs office, we were stopped at the side of the road and the inspection was done on the dirt bank of the roadside. We discovered that we had a little too much ivory by weight, so we gave some to our friends. The officials went through everything in our small trunk and then they hurriedly pushed everything back in because we had to board our plane on time.

We had a treasured family heirloom in the trunk, an antique platter. I had packed it very carefully, but the officers were in a hurry and just replaced it carelessly. When we unpacked at home, we discovered that our treasured platter was broken in several pieces. It was sad but not fatal.

We flew to Bujumbura to the international airport. There we met our friends from Kibagora, the Adamsons. After many years of faithful service, they were returning to the USA to retire. Though we did not realize it at the time, this would also be our last trip. Our two families had planned to make this trip together and visit Egypt and Israel on the way home. We passed through formalities, boarded the plane and took off.

Bujumbura is at the north end of Lake Tanganyika and planes circled over the Lake to gain altitude. Soon I realized that we were not gaining altitude but getting closer and closer to the water. I was a bit frightened, but the plane returned to the airport and personnel there explained the situation. As planes took off, the quality of the fuel was tested. Because such procedure was usually normal, our plane took off a bit early, but the lab radioed that this time the fuel was faulty and had to be replaced before flying on such a long journey. So we all got off and found lodging. It was about three days before the plane was ready and we finally took off again. We were starting another adventure, perhaps the most thrilling of our lives. This had been a very eventful, stressful term, but the wonderful trip home made up for all the dangers and trials. Joy and Len were in the USA, but the three younger girls were with us to share in these adventures.

EGYPT

That evening and night we flew over the desert, north to Egypt. We landed in Cairo where we all stayed at the Lotus Hotel downtown. At breakfast I was wondering about the pyramids. We were seated near a window; I looked out and there in the distance was the Pyramid of Cheops! Soon we set out to visit it close up. We also saw the Temple of the Sun comprised of huge blocks of stone perfectly set together. This was near the Sphinx which we also viewed with awe. Here we had the opportunity for a ride on a camel. Gay mounted one with the help of a guide, but Merry Sue was so nearsighted that she was afraid to be up that high, so she rode a donkey. Leonard and I would have liked to ride a camel, but we were doing this trip on a shoestring and feared spending the money, especially just at the beginning of our trip.

The best part was the pyramid. We walked along one side and then entered. What a thrill to walk along the narrow low hallways to the queen's room, then up to the king's chamber. Here the guides showed us a small opening that went up through the rock layers to the outside. At certain times of the year, a bright star could be seen through this tiny channel. That star must have held a special significance for the pharaoh who had been buried. The ancient builders must have understood a lot about astronomy. The chambers were empty; there was nothing left but the stone bases where the sarcophagi had been. Since childhood I had been told about Egypt and the pyramids but never dreamed I would really get to see one, let alone actually go inside one! What a thrill! If my Grandma could only have known this!

Then we experienced an amazing visit to the great Egyptian museum where the treasures of King Tut were on display. The mummy was encased in gold and jewels and entombed in a small temple of marble with statues of goddesses at the corners. There were also statues of several pharaohs. They all stood with one foot forward and with a typical small beard attached to their chins. There was one of a woman, but she also wore the beard and stood with one foot forward. Perhaps there was a time when there was no male heir and she stepped into the gap, becoming the ruler. It is possible that this happened at the time of the ten plagues in Egypt and the deaths of the firstborn boys. Who knows? This was a statue of Queen Hatchapsut, perhaps the princess that rescued and raised Moses!

What a day of adventures, never to be forgotten by Leonard and me and our three girls. Our great regret was that Joy and Len could not be with us for these great experiences!

The next morning we headed for the airport. Two more airplane adventures were coming to us that day. The first occurred when we found that our plane was a small one labeled "Arab Air Lines." We were a bit apprehensive, wondering what kind of pilots Arabs would be. We were early so we could choose the front seats. After a bit the cockpit door opened and the pilot stepped out. He greeted us, "Hi, y'all," in authentic Texas drawl! We knew we were in good hands!

Soon we were flying above the desert, the "great howling wilderness," the Dead Sea, and other Bible locations. What a thrill to see actual places mentioned in the Bible! Two young women were sitting across the aisle from us, returning from their stint with the Peace Corps. They were not at all interested in the scenery. I wondered how anyone could sit there and read or doze; I thought everyone would consider this a marvelous opportunity.

JERUSALEM AND JORDAN

And then we experienced the second airplane adventure of the day. At the Jerusalem airport I was sitting with Mrs. Adamson, waiting for the formalities to be completed. She looked across the room and mentioned that a woman there looked remarkably like someone she knew, but how could she possibly be in Jerusalem? As we still had to wait longer, she decided to go over and talk with this person. And what do you think? She really did know her! She and her husband were Free Methodist missionaries coming from Japan on furlough. The families had met before at mission conferences in the States.

Their family included two boys and a little girl who was named Bethany. The parents were eager for her to visit her city namesake. We decided that the three families could go about in two groups instead of three. We hired two guides and their taxis to show us the sites of the city and the area on the Jordanian side. This was before the Six-Day War and Jerusalem was strictly divided. Once we had West Jerusalem stamped in our passports, we would not be allowed in the eastern part, so we needed to see the eastern part first.

We saw the tumbled walls of Jericho, drank from Jacob's deep well, viewed the ruins of Ahab's ivory palace, and took a dip in the buoyant Dead Sea. We saw the Jericho Road of the story of the Good Samaritan and the fields below Bethlehem where the shepherds saw and heard the angels announcing the birth of Jesus. We passed by the grave of Rachel, mother of Joseph and Benjamin, who died near Bethlehem giving birth to her younger son. Then we entered the church shielding the spot where, supposedly, Jesus was born. Just to think we were actually there where so many Bible events had occurred and where Jesus had walked, taught and performed miracles! It was blessed and awesome.

The visit to the Garden Tomb was the most amazing, beautiful and sacred of all. It was called Gordon's Tomb because an English general by that name had discovered the site and had it excavated. It was situated outside the city wall just below the hill called Golgotha where many believe the Cross stood. It was in a beautiful garden of flowers, shrubs, large rocks, and the ruins of a wine press. The tomb was cut out of the hillside and contained two rooms; one was the entrance and the other had places for two tombs, one of which apparently had never been used. Before the front wall of the tomb was a low stone wall just far enough from the main wall to make a path for the rolling stone door. How blessed it was to stand there and realize that probably this was the place where Jesus' body was laid and from which He came forth in resurrection victory.

Most people believe that Jesus was crucified on the top of the hill, Golgotha. We were told it was more likely below that hill at the point where two important roads converged. The Romans used crucifixion to discourage any opposition to Rome. They wanted all people to see the punishment and be in subjection rather than risk death. A bus station was located at that site. People and buses constantly passed. Imagine such a sacred spot, yet people came and went with no thought that Jesus died there for the sins of the world.

Then we ascended the Mount of Olives and visited the Church of the Ascension and the spot from which, it is thought, Jesus ascended to heaven. A highlight of the day for little Bethany was visiting the village of Bethany where Mary and Martha and their brother Lazarus lived. This was the place where Lazarus died and Jesus raised him to life again. Little Bethany was excited to see it.

JERUSALEM, ISRAEL

The next day we entered Jewish Jerusalem, passing through the Mendlebaum Gate and going through customs as in a foreign country.

We visited many sacred sites. As I can't remember which site was on which side of divided Jerusalem, I'll mention them all together. We saw the Temple Mount where the Dome of the Rock, the famous Muslim Mosque, stood. We had to remove our shoes upon entering. Close by was the Wailing Wall where the Jews pray for their country and the peace of Jerusalem. We also saw the Pool of Siloam where Jesus healed a blind man.

We visited Zion, the city of David, and the Upper Room where Jesus and His disciples met for the Last Supper. A Jewish rabbi gave us a blessing there. I wanted to tell him that we should have given him a blessing, for we could have blessed him in the name of Jesus whom the Jews still reject.

We passed by more sacred places or sites of ancient ruins, including Pilate's Judgment Hall and the Via Dolorosa, the way to the Cross. The Catholic Church designates another place as Jesus' tomb, but many Protestants prefer to think it was the Garden Tomb outside the city. More of the details for that location correspond to those given in the Bible.

While we were there, we saw the preparation on Friday afternoon for the Sabbath. We saw many orthodox Jewish men, with large black hats and side curls. They were carrying small bundles and hurrying along the streets. They were going to the public baths to wash clean for the Sabbath and were required to be home by sunset. On the Sabbath which was our Saturday, we attended a synagogue where women and children were seated in the rear balcony. I was amazed at the irreverence shown by the male congregation. Several times the cantor, who was facing the sacred scrolls, turned around and admonished them. I thought this was a sign that their hearts were not in true worship of God and they were only following a set of rules.

We had parted with the Adamsons and the other family when we entered West Jerusalem. They had planned to visit other places including Lebanon. We took a taxi on Sunday up the sea coast to Mount Carmel where Elijah defeated the priests of Baal. It was a beautiful city built high on a hill overlooking the Mediterranean. We stayed that night in a bed and breakfast house.

Early the next morning we traveled east on a bus with other tourists. Our tour guide was a Jew named Paul who told us many things along the way. We visited Nazareth where Jesus grew up and also the house that is thought to have been Joseph's. It was a cave below the street with bunk beds and grain bins carved out of the rock. Supposedly, he had his carpenter shop up above on street level. I was appalled to think of the family living that way. I bought a small olivewood vase to remember such an important place. Nazareth was built high on a hill; we could understand how Jesus was nearly pushed off a cliff there.

Then we headed for the Sea of Galilee. How wonderful to be right there where Jesus spent so much of His ministry. In Capernaum we saw the pillars and ruins of an early Christian church and a collection of huge millstones used for grinding grain into flour. Some of these were designed to be operated by hand labor; others were arranged so that oxen could operate the mill by walking around and around.

At noon the other tourists went to a nice hotel for dinner but we wanted to see more of the Sea of Galilee. We sat on a pier and ate the simple lunch we had brought. It was mainly special Jewish bread and roasted green almonds which were delicious. Though we were a bit hungry, it was well worth it to look across the beautiful Sea of Galilee. We walked up the hill in time for the bus and rode back to Carmel. What a day!

Our time in Israel was nearly up, so the next day we journeyed south along the Mediterranean coast to Israel's big city, Tel Aviv. We spent some time on the beach. We looked south down the coast and could dimly see the city of Joppa where Peter had spent some time with Simon the Tanner and had raised Dorcas back to life. We had a good night at a nice seaside hotel. The taxi we had hired for the next morning came later than we expected, so we were a little late and worried about reaching our plane in time. Then we hit a serious traffic jam! A young police woman was called and she straightened things out in a jiffy. We arrived in time to board a big El Al plane for Europe. What great adventures we had had in Egypt and Israel, but still more adventures awaited us on our way home!

ATHENS, GREECE

Our first stop was Athens. There was a little time there for refueling, so we grabbed a taxi to downtown Athens. Though we had such a short time, still we could see the columns and ruins of the Acropolis high on a hill just beyond the city streets. Then we could say we had been in Greece. Next we flew up the east coast of Italy and saw the cities along the shore including Venice. About then, Melodie and I took a trip to the restroom. When we came out, we looked down and there, suddenly, we were over the majestic, snow-clad Alps. What a sight!

SWITZERLAND

We landed at Bern and took a train for Lausanne on Lake Geneva. Our very good Swiss friends, the Andres, lived there, but they were away just then. Mr. Andre had arranged places for us at a Swiss Bible school high up the mountain. We rode a cable car, a funicular, up to the school. I remember the mountain sides covered with flowers, including gentians, bright yellow flowers, and edelweiss. It was still early spring so the cozy feather beds felt wonderful. Swiss breakfasts were very good with special bread, maybe some prepared meat, cheese, jam and coffee. A Bible conference was in progress so Leonard and I heard some good Bible messages in French. As a special treat, we rode the ski lift up to the very top of that mountain; it was scary! I had Melodie with me, Leonard had Gay, and poor Merry Sue, as the oldest, had a seat by herself between the other two. She did very well.

Our next stop was Lausanne where Mr. Andre had obtained tickets for us to attend the Swiss National Fair; it was like a world's fair, only for just the one country. This was only held every twenty years, so we were fortunate to have been there at that time. I remember most a huge perpetual motion machine without a motor, yet constantly moving balls along a track. Also, the exhibit of huge Swiss cows amazed me. Then we watched a program of school children. Groups from each canton (state), wearing the costumes of their canton, performed folk dances which were very pretty.

We were grateful to the Andres for making these experiences possible for us. Next we took a train ride to the capitol, Geneva. There we stayed overnight at a youth hostel at the top of a rather tall building. The next morning we boarded the plane for the USA. After refueling at Lisbon, we struck out across the Atlantic. As we took off from Portugal, I noticed the huge rocks facing the sea, and so we bid Europe good-bye.

NEW YORK, USA

We landed safely in New York City about seven hours later where the World's Fair was in progress. We spent the night at a mission home on the New Jersey side, but the next morning we took a bus to visit the Fair. It was awesome; we could have spent a week at the Fair and still not seen everything. We returned to our motel, happy but very weary.

From New York to St. Louis was a routine flight but, on landing, we met our son Len (Leonard Leigh). A happy reunion! We had not seen him for about two years. He had graduated from high school and learned to drive in the city. Our mission headquarters was in St. Louis, so we reported in and stayed a day or two. We managed to get a car and then drove to Omaha, with Len, to see Joy. When we had left four years before, she had been ready for her senior year in high school. Now she was graduating from nursing school.

We arrived at the hospital where she had trained and were ushered into a pleasant waiting room while Joy was told of our arrival. We could hardly wait until she could come from her classes. We were so happy to be with her again! She showed us about the hospital and then we found a motel to await the great Graduation Day. It was a lovely service; Joy sang in a group of classmates. She received special recognition as one of the best in her class. We were very proud of her! And now, at last, we felt that we were home!

The next business was finding a place to live during furlough. Since the family that had sponsored Joy lived in Lincoln near Omaha, we visited them a few days and looked for a house to rent. We found a very nice old-fashioned house near our friends, the Lotts. It was also right across the street from the pastor of our Berean Church. Next, Len and I each found a job at a hospital where I became night nurse. And thus our furlough began.

THIRD FURLOUGH

After all our thrilling travels and Joy's graduation, we were ready to settle down for awhile. We chose to live in Lincoln, Nebraska. Some friends loaned us sufficient furniture. We went to a secondhand store and bought enough dishes and pots to get along. We unpacked the things we had brought in our trunk and proceeded to make a home. Schooling for the family had to be arranged. Joy continued advanced nursing school in Omaha, and Len was attending university classes in Lincoln. Merry Sue was in high school, Gay attended junior high, and Melodie was in elementary. I don't remember how we arranged transportation for all, but the lower schools were all in our area.

We had a number of friends working at the Back to the Bible Broadcast and at the church. The situation was pleasant and offered good activities for all of us. Leonard was often away from home, working on mission projects and visiting churches. When he was home, he fixed up a place in the attic of this big house where I could sleep days. We were all busy and happy.

I remember one day at noon when Melodie came home from school, crying. I probed for the reason and she said, "This afternoon we have to draw a bird and I don't know how to draw a bird." I showed her how to draw a very simple picture, using an oval for the body, two sticks for legs, a small circle for the head, and a sharp V for the beak. She went back to school quite happy. We also attended a musical program and a swimming exhibition at Sue's school. Melodie learned to swim that summer in a Red Cross program. Altogether, it was a pleasant furlough, but the time was coming when we had to decide our next step.

Affairs back in Congo were very unsettled and unsafe, especially for teenaged girls. It did not seem wise to take our family back there at this time. At the annual conference of our mission, it was decided to send us to work with Navajo Indians at Thoreau, New Mexico. One family, the Marshalls, were doing a good work there, including church services and Sunday School, visitation and language classes, but they could use a little help. So our furlough was ended and we began a new stage of our work for the Lord through Berean Mission, not in Congo but in New Mexico.

OUR 3 YOUNGER GIRLS WITH
RWANDAN TEACHER

MELODIE & BURUNDI GIRLS

BALEGA BRIDES. THEY MADE
THEIR TOPS

BURUNDI GIRLS IN DRESSES THEY
PLANNED AND MADE

READY TO TRAVEL - STUDEBAKER PICKUP
"STEW-DEE-BA-KAY"

IN THE DITCH DUE TO SLIPPERY ROAD

CROSSING THE EQUATOR – LEONARD & 4
OLDER CHILDREN

PYRAMID NEAR CAIRO

CHAPTER FOURTEEN

LIFE BACK IN THE USA

It had been a wonderful, once-in-a-lifetime trip. We had experienced and seen things we had only dreamed about. This trip was off to a sad start, leaving our Balega friends and the missionaries for an indefinite time, but a joyous ending as we rejoined our daughter Joy just in time for her graduation.

The first thirty-two years of my life were spent in Tulsa, Western Colorado, and Denver. Then we went to Congo, spending about twenty years in that work. Now we were going to work with Navajo Indians in New Mexico. We moved to a small town, Thoreau, just east of the Continental Divide. We settled in a small mission house and began to get acquainted with the resident missionaries, the Navajos, and our new surroundings in the Southwest.

New Mexico is known as the Land of Enchantment; the rock formations, the mountains, and the evergreen trees were beautiful but very different from our lush jungle country. The people were also very different. The Africans were very friendly, open and expressive; the Indians were self-contained and did not readily express their emotions. It was hard for us to get to know them. Then, too, we did not know their language. Our senior missionary, Mr. Marshall, did very well and tried to teach us some Navajo which is a difficult language. Most of the Navajo in Thoreau spoke at least some English.

School for the girls was always a serious consideration. Sue took a bus to the high school in Gallop, the next city. Gay and Melodie attended the local Thoreau school, Gay in middle school and Melodie in elementary. Gay was required to take a foreign language course. There we were where Spanish was freely spoken, but she chose German. I don't think she went very far in it. The Marshall family had five girls (and a baby boy) so there were plenty of companions.

We tried to help where we could. I taught a Sunday School class of mixed Navajos and white older children. Leonard helped a great deal with the manual labor and visitation. He and I went to a nearby town each week and taught Bible lessons to school children. An older Navajo woman came often to our house for a visit. We had good times together though neither spoke the other's language.

The Navajos had serious social problems. Many still followed their ancient, spirit-worship religion which often included native drugs. Alcohol addiction was frequent and poverty, lack of motivation, and lack of jobs compounded the situation. There was probably resentment against the white people for taking their land away from them. Though they were so different from the Africans, both peoples had great spiritual problems. We wanted to tell them about God's love and the salvation He provided for all people. The work was difficult; they were imbued with their ancient ways and were slow to change. Often we felt we were getting nowhere. In the 1990's, however, after forty years of ministry by Berean and other missions, missionaries began to see results from our early work. They were training Navajo Christian pastors and workers to reach their own people.

So we settled into life in the Southwest. In addition to our mission work, we visited other Berean locations in the state. We enjoyed picnics in the mountains or by a lake and visited old Indian ruins and modern pueblos. It was all very different but interesting.

We had two memorable occasions. One was at Christmas when Joy and Len came to visit. Len had graduated from Greenville College and was studying and working in St. Louis. Joy was studying and working in Omaha, but they managed to both come on the same train. We met them in the next town late at night, but it was a joyous reunion. I remember that we had a big pot of clam chowder waiting when we returned home. We had a lovely Christmas together for a few days, but then they had to go back to their own activities.

The other occasion was when we had a good snow, about six inches. My fourth sister, Pat, her husband, and her three children came from San Bernardino where it never snows. The kids had a great time building a snowman and throwing snowballs. Pat's husband worked for the railroad so they could easily get passes for the family. It was so good to see my sister and her husband, and it was great for our children to get to visit with their cousins. Then in the summer, Pat and her family and another sister, Mary, from San Diego, had a great family camp out on the desert and invited our three girls. What an experience with all those children together, ten in all. It was a wonderful opportunity for our children to visit with relatives they had only heard about.

Our year in New Mexico was over. We didn't feel we were doing much good there. We decided it was time to leave the mission and get secular jobs to earn our living. We visited friends who lived near Hutchinson, Kansas, where they pastored a little church. The husband had been a classmate from DBI and a fellow missionary in Congo. He helped Leonard find a position in a Christian School (K-12) in Hutchinson. Leonard taught some Bible classes, drove the school bus, and helped out where needed.

I well remember the day we moved from New Mexico to Kansas. Joy had been with us a few days. Leonard and some men had loaded a rented pickup the evening before. He started out quite early so as to have the house we had rented ready for us by night. All four of our girls were there and that made five in the car, but we still could pack in the remaining smaller things. We had previously visited Chaco Canyon and wanted Joy to see it also. It is a place of many Anastazi ruins, even a large ancient pueblo. This was a bit out of the way but well worth it. We drove on to Albuquerque and then headed north. We drove for hours and hours and finally arrived in Hutchinson long after midnight; we were all very tired. Leonard had moved most of our things into the house and had it open for us. We made beds on the floor or wherever and slept the rest of the night!

As usual, school was a problem; however, schools were not far away. It was Sue's last year in high school, and we thought the Christian school would be good for her. Gay went to the local high school and Melodie was still in elementary. We got them all settled and then I got a job at a nursing home. Church people loaned us some furniture and we managed well. We enjoyed church and school activities. Merry Sue graduated from high school, the second in her class. The other girls were doing well too.

Sadly, after that year, the Christian school no longer needed Leonard so we were again looking for a place. The director of the home where I worked was offered a position as a director of a fine new nursing home in nearby Wichita. He invited me to come with him to be a nurse there. Also, Leonard could work there as maintenance man. We prayed about this and decided to move to Wichita where we both had jobs. What was needed was a night nurse, so that was my work. Someone was supposed to work the first night with me, but nobody showed up. So there I was, in a new situation and a responsible position and had no one to give me guidance. I pretty well knew the night routine, so I managed fairly well. After a few months, however, I became very weary of night duty. I was never able to get enough sleep in the daytime.

Leonard was doing well with the maintenance work, keeping the building clean, overseeing the landscaping, and keeping track of the many walkers, canes and wheelchairs. Since I was working nights and he, days, sometimes I would pass him coming to work on his bicycle as I drove home.

I looked for day work and landed in a large Catholic hospital in the intensive care facility. I don't know why I was put in that responsible position. I was a nurse from the African jungle with little hospital experience. At first I was terrified. I would go to work and then stand before the door praying, "Dear Lord, do I really have to enter that door and go to work?" After a time, however, I grew to enjoy the work very much. I learned many new things and got along okay. I enjoyed working with the other nurses. Now, after about thirty years, I still keep in touch with two of my former coworkers.

At first we rented a little house, but then the owners wanted it back. Nearby we found a larger house to rent. On the coldest, windiest day of the winter in January, we moved into our more convenient three-bedroom house. That gave us, Gay, and Melodie each a room. I fixed up a nice room in the basement for Sue to use when she was home.

There was the school problem again! Sue had graduated from high school and was ready for college. We lived near Friends University and we thought it would be good for Sue to have the experience of living in a dorm with other girls, so she moved to the university. Gay was a junior in high school and Melodie attended middle school at Mayberry

Junior High. I wonder how we managed transportation for all this. We figured it out all right, but I can't remember how. It was at Mayberry that Melodie sang her first solo. The school drama department was presenting excerpts from *South Pacific* and she sang the song, "I'm in Love." She did very well. After that, we arranged voice lessons for her and also insisted that she take elementary piano lessons.

The years we spent there were very eventful for our girls; it was a strategic time in their lives. Gay met a girl in school who was unhappy with her situation. Her parents had divorced and she was living with an aunt. Gay invited her to share her room and this worked out well. She had a part-time job and her own car so that helped Gay get to school. She also had a boyfriend and all three girls were developing more associations with the guys. Thus, we were happy to have Betty Troutman with us and "adopted" her into our family. We will see more of her in this story.

About the same time, we also "adopted" another young lady who had become a friend of Joy's. Her name was Bonni Baker. Joy took her under her care and they worked and lived together several years. We consider her our daughter like the other girls. Joy was taking a course in midwifery at Johns Hopkins Medical School in Baltimore, Maryland, and Bonni was studying to be a medical technician at the same school.

They each finished the course, lived together and worked a year in Baltimore. Later, they worked in Omaha, Kansas City, and Dallas.

Soon we became known in the neighborhood as the family with "all those girls and the boyfriends coming and going." That summer Gay had an assortment of boyfriends. I didn't think much of any of them, but one day she met another fellow. She told me that he was very nice, played the accordion and had red hair. I said, "We'll take him!" and we did. That fall, her senior year in high school, she became engaged to Jim Arthur.

Merry Sue was becoming interested in Gil Goodger. It came about this way. After a year of college, she wanted to do something else. She became interested in computers and was admitted to a school to train operators. This was just the beginning of the computer age. The school's computer was housed in a metal tunnel about seven feet long which they called the Great Red Monster. (Now I am using a little pink instrument about ten by fifteen inches! Computers have come a long way in a short time.)

After Sue completed computer school, she got a job in the hospital at the records and computer office. It was night work and involved printing and delivering reports to all the floors. A young man working as a respiratory therapist was called all over the hospital as the need arose in the night. Sue and this young man often met in the corridors and became acquainted as she delivered reports and he gave treatments. They found they had many things in common and this resulted in an engagement. So we added two fellows to our family associations.

By this time, Len had graduated from Greenville College. He wanted to become a physician and was studying medicine in Guadalajara, Mexico. There they said he spoke Spanish with a French accent. This he had acquired during our stay in Belgium.

Sometime along here, Joy had surgery for cancer of the thyroid gland. (She has had no more trouble from it since, for which we do thank God.) Later, she was involved in a car accident which gave her a serious back injury. It was months before she fully recovered. Between these two health issues, it was best that she not go to a foreign country to serve the Lord. She did professional nursing for a time. Then she took the position of children's minister in a small urban church. Most of the children were from unstable families who moved often. The children were behind in school. Whites, blacks and Hispanics, they all needed help. Joy did not need to cross an ocean to be a missionary. She taught Bible stories, songs, and the love of our strong, dependable, loving God. She engaged a number of volunteer tutors to help the children with their school work. Leonard and I helped with the tutoring and enjoyed getting acquainted with some of the kids.

Gay and Betty graduated from high school that spring. Gay got a job at the telephone company. Jim had gone to Denver to further his accordion expertise. Meanwhile, Jim had met some students from Western Bible College, an offshoot of DBI, and liked their fellowship and teachings. He felt spiritual training was even more important than his music, so he changed schools.

Gay and Jim were married that Christmas in 1969. Though she was our fourth child, she was the first to marry. Jim's parents attended a large Presbyterian church and wanted to have the wedding there. Gay had a beautiful service. I was working full-time at the hospital, but I managed to make a lovely white satin gown with lace inserts and seed pearls. The four bridesmaids' gowns were purple satin. I also made her a going-away dress and a plaid coat and tam.

They bought a small mobile home and set it up in a trailer park in a resort area just west of the city. It was fairly close to Jim's school. Gay could transfer her job to the same telephone company in Denver. Beside her work, she was able to sing in a school choral group and take a class or two. Because the mobile home was so small, they bought a prefab room to add to the trailer. Leonard and I went to help put it together. We slept in a tent for a week or so. There was some project that required work on the roof. As I was the smallest, they put me on the roof, driving in screws with an electric drill (my first and only construction job). Why do you suppose they needed another room? Our first grandchild, William Patrick Arthur, was born in November after his parents had been married almost two years.

Not to be outdone by her younger sister, Merry Sue and Gil Goodger were married about six months later. Sue didn't care for an elaborate wedding so they were married in our small Bible church. She made her own white lace gown and baked their wedding cake. The service was very simple with our pastor officiating. I think I made her going-away dress. Sue and Gil left that very evening to drive back to Omaha where Gil was working. It was not long until they had a son, Titus, about six weeks after Will was born.

While I was working in Wichita, my stepfamily, consisting of my mother, stepfather and half-siblings and their families, planned a family reunion in Eastern Washington. Melodie, Leonard and I drove there. Because we did not have much time, we drove right through, night and day. One drove, one slept, and the other was supposed to keep the driver awake. We were quite sleepy when we got there but had a great time with two of my sisters, my brother and their families. Merry Sue and my sister Mary came from Arizona also. I had not seen my mother for some years so it was great to see her and meet my stepfather, Dean Baker. My father died when I was a year old. My first stepfather had been dead about three years when Mother met this good Christian man and married him. I saw him at two occasions and would have liked to have had the opportunity to know him better.

Our family was getting smaller. Joy and Len were grown and gone, Gay was married and in Denver, and Merry Sue was married and lived in Omaha. We had been paying rent for several years and had nothing to show for it. We decided to buy a mobile home. We found a nice new one and stationed it in a new park south of town. Melodie finished high school near the top of her class. Then she decided to become a dental hygienist and took a course at the university. When she graduated, Gay's friend Betty was also graduating from the nursing school at the top of her class. She was an R.N. and then married a physician. She decided to train to be a doctor, and guess what? She is my primary care physician today.

Len had taken some medical courses in Mexico and some seminary courses in St. Louis. He was studying at a Lutheran college. While there he met Angie K. and they fell in love. He and Angie met over the telephone through a special program the Lutheran church was conducting. Len and Angie were married in a small Lutheran church. Our mission headquarters was in St. Louis and our president took part in the ceremony. All the family drove there for the occasion except Joy who had just been injured in a car accident. Joy had declared that nothing was going to keep her from attending her brother's wedding! We got to meet Angie's family. Len was trying to decide whether he wanted to become a minister or a doctor. They lived in St. Louis for a time and later moved to Wichita where he completed courses to become a physician's assistant. Then they had a baby girl, Krisinda. Len worked in the veterans' hospital in Wichita.

MY MOST TERRIBLE DAY

It was over thirty years ago, but I have yet to experience a worse one. I went to the hospital as usual and was assigned to my work. Then the cardiac care floor asked for help and I was sent there. I reported upstairs but was told they didn't need me after all. I returned and started my work in intensive care. Soon, however, cardiac care decided they really did want me. Arriving up there, I was assigned two difficult patients. I struggled all day to give proper care to the two patients and keep all the schedules. At last, that work day was finished.

Len's wife was taking some university courses; therefore, she put the baby in a nursery near my work. It was my chore to pick her up and take her home. I really enjoyed doing this. I delivered her safely (one good thing for that day). I was to pick up my husband at a doctor's office. Plans were not settled and I needed to get in touch with him. I phoned home, but daughter Melodie, as most teenagers, was calling her friends, so I decided to check at his workplace.

When I left Len's house, it started to sprinkle and then rain hard. I drove on and then my windshield wipers stopped working! There was no news of Leonard at his workplace, so I carefully drove home through the rain. There I found out that Leonard was waiting for me at the doctor's office at the other end of town, about sixty blocks away. I took our other car, which happened to be there, hoping its wipers would work. I resumed my travels, drove a few blocks, and ran out of gas! So I slogged through the rain three blocks to a filling station, bought a can of gas and carried it back to the car. After some difficulty, I got the car started and then drove to return the gas can. Driving on, I finally arrived at the doctor's office. Rejoicing that I had made it, I entered and looked about. Leonard was not there! This was the last straw; I returned to the parking lot, sat down in the car and cried! I didn't know where Leonard had been, perhaps trying to call me. I didn't know what else to do. Just then Leonard came to the parking lot and recognized his car. We were certainly glad to find each other, at last! Finally success! Though I have had many troubles in my life, never have I had another such day. Many years later we moved to a location near that office and as I drive by, I always think of that Most Terrible Day.

CHAPTER FIFTEEN

LIFE IN ARKANSAS

After seven or eight years in Wichita, Leonard looked for a position in some form of Christian work. He was studying a correspondence course in accounting in order to be more helpful. After some search, he was employed as business manager at Citadel Bible College in Ozark, Arkansas. We sold our mobile home and found another in an interesting location just outside Ozark. It was on a wooded lot behind a hill from the busy road. It was not a long drive to his work and the little town. The school was situated on a high bluff overlooking the Arkansas River, a beautiful view. Citadel Bible was a small college, serving about 100 students.

We had some enjoyable experiences during the eight years we lived there. It was a joy to meet the instructors and students at school, as well as a number of the townspeople. Leonard drove up the hill each day to his office and I found a job at the local forty-bed hospital. Sundays we drove about thirty miles to Clarksville, the next town, where Leonard pastored a small Bible Church. If I had had to work Saturday night, I would take a pillow and sleep on the way to church. Sometimes we stayed the afternoon, calling on the local people, inviting them to church, and talking about God's blessings. Sunday evenings we frequently visited other small churches in the area where some of the college students did the preaching.

One of my experiences was an accidental meeting with an old friend. The college was interdenominational but there were several churches of various denominations in the town. One was a Free Methodist Church which had been without a pastor for some time. Then a new pastor and his wife were assigned there. Somehow they learned about us and that we had worked in Africa. We soon found out an amazing fact! The pastor's wife was Katherine Hendricks, our girls' teacher when they attended the mission school at Mweya, Burundi. It was amazing that we should meet again in a small town in Arkansas. We had some good times reminiscing and visiting together.

A missionary family came to the school. They had been missionaries in Colombia and had had some dangerous experiences. Two of their children were students in the school. The father taught Bible classes in the school and also night classes for townspeople. The family across the road from us did not seem to have a very good reputation in the neighborhood. I invited the woman to come to the Bible classes with us and she accepted! I was sure she did not have much Bible knowledge so I suggested that we study the lessons together. We had many good times and she became a very good friend. I could tell she was growing in "grace and knowledge of the Lord" and I rejoiced. Even after we moved away we kept in touch with each other.

There we had another good experience. The college decided to start a Christian elementary school. The sister of one of the college professors had received training as a teacher and was eager to start such a school. I was interested and volunteered to help. I had taught my own children primary grades in Congo so had gained some experience. In preparation for teaching, I took a week's course at a college in Pensacola, Florida, which I found very helpful. There I was introduced to the study of phonics. So I resigned from the hospital and became a kindergarten teacher. Sometimes I worked weekends as a nurse.

While in the area, Leonard and I took several trips, just the two of us, to see the sights of beautiful Arkansas. We enjoyed the mountains, canyons, and caves. Once we went to Eureka Springs late in October. A crafts convention was in town and all the hotel and motel rooms were taken. We finally found a room at a bed and breakfast. The hostess there said, "I suppose you want to see the Passion Play." We were surprised because we thought the season was over. She told us that that was the last night and she could get tickets if we wished. Of course we considered this a special treat for our trip, but we would be cold, sitting out on those hard bleachers. She thoughtfully loaned us a blanket and four brown grocery bags. These bags were to put our feet in for a little warmth. This was our first time to view the play which was a graphic production of what Jesus had suffered for us. We saw it another time later when some of our children and grandchildren could come too.

After three, four or five years, Leonard went to an oculist in Fort Smith and was given new glasses. Soon after that he complained that these glasses were not helping. That eye doctor thought he needed cataract surgery so we tried that. Still, it did not help much. As an accountant, he had to be able to identify numbers but it was becoming more and more difficult, so he decided to retire. I retired from the hospital and school and we moved back to Wichita.

Before this, Joy had taken a Bible course in Phoenix at Arizona School of the Bible. Though she had had one year of classes at Grace Bible College in Omaha, it was deemed best that she have more Bible training. While there, she met a fellow student, a young man from Hawaii of Japanese descent, Dennis Domen. They had many experiences together that year and became good friends. Then Joy went to Baltimore and took a course in midwifery, but the two kept in touch. He was then studying in a seminary in California. They met in Albuquerque for vacation and became engaged. We were living in Arkansas at that time. Joy was working at a hospital in Wichita. Dennis was moving to Wichita from California. Joy brought him to Ozark to meet us. We were pleased with her choice. I remember he said that he didn't understand how people could live so far from the ocean.

At that time, Melodie had completed her classes to become a dental hygienist. She was working with a dentist in Hays, Kansas, her first professional position. She had met a handsome young man, Dan Page, who worked in heavy construction. They became friends and were engaged. After Melodie had worked there for several months, they decided to be married. They wanted a very simple wedding and so were married in her sister Gay's living room in Newton, Kansas. Gay's pastor officiated. Dan and Melodie went back to Hays for a time. Later, she worked in Arkansas, Oklahoma, and in Hesston and Wichita, Kansas. Dan could get jobs anywhere.

Joy had completed nurse's training, two years of Bible college, some postgrad nursing courses, and a professional midwifery course at Johns Hopkins, Baltimore. Now she was working as a supervising nurse in labor and delivery. Meanwhile, Dennis had completed a seminary course in California. He came to Wichita and they were married in a city park where they had reserved a pavilion. It was a lovely fall day in late October 1978, except for the Kansas wind. Some of our decorations blew away.

Joy had prepared the cake and food ahead of time. Folding chairs were set up on the lawn. Joy's pastor performed the ceremony. His family and our family had been friends in St. Louis for some time. Dennis had a brother studying in Washington and he and his wife came and also Denny's mother came from Honolulu. Joy's dress was very special; it had been my grandmother's Sunday-go-to-meeting white summer dress. Grandma had done a lot of white embroidery and many tiny tucks. I altered it a bit and Joy looked lovely in it. (She still has it; now it is probably about 130 years old.) After a short but delightful wedding trip, Joy returned to her nursing work and Denny to his work as a counselor in a county program to help kids who had gotten in trouble. He studied for his master's degree in counseling and continued his work to rescue troubled youths.

A year or two before this, Joy and Bonni had been living in the Dallas area. They moved back to Wichita, buying a house in the south part of the city. Bonni had married in Dallas and had a baby son. Her marriage did not work out so it was good she had a place with Joy. When Joy married, Bonni got her own small house.

In due time, Joy and Denny's son Christopher was born. Len and Angie were in Wichita with their little daughter, Krisinda. He was finishing a course to become a physician's assistant. Gay and Jim and little Will had added a baby daughter, Nicole, to the family. They were living in Newton, just north of Wichita, where Jim was chief announcer for the Christian radio station, KJRG. Merry and Gil and little Titus were living in Topeka near his parents where Gil was a postal service employee. Melodie had married Dan and worked as a dental hygienist in Oklahoma. Then they moved back to the Wichita area near her sisters. She found a good position in a dental office in Hesston, a small town north of Wichita. Dan was working in heavy construction in various places.

Len had finished his physician's assistant course at Wichita State University. He was working as an assistant to a surgeon at the veterans' hospital. We were still living in Arkansas. One Sunday evening we were at church when a telephone call came through for us. We were told that our son Len had had an accident and sustained a serious wound to the head. We were much alarmed and went to our home and waited for further news. The pastor and a number of friends from church came to sustain us. We waited tensely for some time and then came the call that our son had died. That was a terrible shock and great sorrow.

We immediately set out for Wichita, driving most of the night. We just wanted to be near our daughters and especially Len's wife Angie and daughter Krisinda. A lovely service was held for him at the Lutheran church where they attended and many people commented about how he had ministered to them. He is buried in Wichita. Angie chose a simple plaque for him saying, "Yahweh called me," Yahweh being a special name for God.

CHAPTER SIXTEEN

RETIREMENT

It was not long after this tragedy that Leonard could no longer do accounting work. So he resigned from the school and applied for Social Security. It was a bit early but worked out well, as we could collect allotments for Melodie's continuing education. At that time she was still in school studying to become a dental hygienist. We decided to move back to the Wichita area. Gay and Jim and family were still in Newton; Joy and Denny and Bonni were in Wichita. We looked for a mobile home in the area and bought one in Hesston where Melodie was working. By that time Melodie and Dan were married. Their mobile home was parked on one side of town and ours on the extreme other side, about two miles apart. They were able to move their mobile home right next door to ours. This was surely nice for both families and so began a happy, interesting time in Hesston. We were where we could easily visit most of our family.

Leonard could not get a Kansas driver's license because of his eyes. Then I had to do all our driving. At that time we were driving a car with standard shift. We had gotten it just as Melodie was learning to drive; we had thought it well for her to learn gearshift driving first, so we bought that type of car. Later, however, I broke my right wrist and could not do the shifting. This did not keep us quietly at home. I did the foot pedal part and Leonard did the hand shifting. We managed safely, but the police probably would not have approved.

While Melodie was our next-door neighbor, we developed a pleasant custom. About 6:00 a.m. Melodie would call us and we would all go for a brisk walk. To accompany us were her two dogs, our dog, the neighbor's dog, and an ambitious cat. We all walked along our country road to a little stream and back. It made a pleasant and energizing start for the day.

Leonard's eyes were failing. We found an excellent oculist in Wichita and made many trips to see him. Over time, Leonard received six corneal transplants, three on each eye, one after another. Five of them failed. Though he could not see well, he constructed a back deck for our mobile home. It was screened-in and made a good entrance as well as dining area and workplace in the summer. He obtained most of the material by collecting boards from the city dump.

Soon after we moved there, I was invited to teach Bible classes with Stonecroft Ministries. At first I declined. Then I remembered our teacher at Ozark. He had urged us to share our knowledge of the Bible which we had acquired back in Bible school. I taught several classes in Hesston and Newton. I enjoyed this very much and it gave me opportunity to meet many people. We found a good Mennonite church whose pastor was schooled at Grace Bible College in Omaha, the same school Joy had attended. Ours was a small church in the country near three towns, thus serving a wide area.

One of my adventures there was to help with Vacation Bible School. A friend and I devised a whole week's program in which the kids actually did many of the things we were teaching. It was about the Children of Israel leaving Egypt and traveling to the Promised Land. The children made mud bricks for Pharaoh, unleavened bread, woven paper baskets, small clay lamps, and a model tabernacle. We divided the whole group into the twelve tribes of Israel. But that was too much to handle, so each group had to be two tribes. The last day they crossed Jordan, entered the Promised Land, and found their tribal allotments.

All through her teenage years, Melodie had been trying to lose weight, so after her marriage she took a Weight Watcher's course and got down to just the right size. Then she got pregnant! Their son Anthony was born in Newton, the day the Desert Storm War began, January 17, 1991. She continued to be a bit heavy for years. Then I had a chance to visit her in Denver; I had not seen her for several months. When we arrived, she came out to the car and I was amazed. I said, "I think you are my daughter, but where is the rest of you?" She has been a nice size ever since. She goes to Tai Kwando classes and is, at present, only one belt away from the coveted black belt.

A sad situation then came about. The radio station, to cut down expenses, decided to fire Jim and replace him with someone for a lower salary. This left Jim high and dry. Both he and Gay tried to find work but it was difficult. Gay did some housecleaning for others. They had both been interested in missionary work, so they figured this was a good time to investigate opportunities. They applied to the Mennonite Brethren Mission and were accepted to minister in Brazil. They completed two terms there, partly in Sao Paulo and partly way back in the interior at Campo Grande. Will and Nicole attended a large international school in San Paulo, Pan American Christian Academy (PACA) and they each graduated from high school there.

They were just ready to return home for furlough when, suddenly, Jim died in Sao Paulo, perhaps from a heart attack or an acute allergic attack. The children both had returned to the USA and Gay came back, as planned. What should she do next? She took some college courses, mainly in English. Then she returned to Sao Paulo as a teacher of English as a second language. In the church with which they had been working was a very helpful young Christian man, Paulo. After Gay returned to Brazil, they were married and Sao Paulo has been her home ever since. She is known as Ruthe Cavalcante there. She has flown back several times to have a visit with her daughter and son, her sisters and me.

Will had graduated from Wheaton University in Chicago. One of my nephews was working in Chicago at that time, so we had a delightful visit with him and his family, as well as having a convenient place to stay while attending Will's graduation. Several years later, Nicole graduated from Colorado Christian University in Denver. It was an extension of Denver Bible Institute where Leonard and I had attended. We were glad we were able to see her graduation, especially since we could not attend the high school graduation ceremonies of our own son Len and daughter Joy.

Anthony, Melodie's son, was born early in 1991 and they had moved to Wichita. We helped them quite a bit as Melodie had to go back to work soon. Gay and family were ministering in Brazil at that time. Merry, Gil and son had moved to Southeast Kansas. Joy, Denny and son; Len's wife and daughter; and Bonni and son were all living in Wichita. That left Leonard and me, on our own, about an hour's drive away from the others.

Then one day a strong tornado ripped right through our little town of Hesston. It did a lot of damage to buildings and other property in its narrow sweep through town. There were no physical injuries in Hesston; Joy had called to urge us to seek shelter. We were living in a mobile home which was more vulnerable in such storms. We took refuge in a very heavy, strong storage shed. We heard it coming like a freight train but were about a mile away from the direct path. We lost electricity and phone power, and our water pump couldn't work. We hurried to the next town to phone Joy that we were okay and to buy water; we were thankful to be spared. We spent the next week helping some of our friends clean up the mess the storm had brought to their homes.

It was the Lord's protection that as the tornado swept right through the town, strategic services were spared: police, fire station, pharmacy, and grocery store.

Melodie was working in the medical building. Those working there went to the basement to wait. Lights went out. They were seated at a table. Melodie asked, "Does anyone want to hold my hand?" Immediately, she felt six or seven hands touching her. We were thankful that building, too, was spared. It was really near the town's water tower. If the tornado had struck that, it would have fallen right on Melodie's building.

After that storm, Joy and Denny were concerned about our living this distance from the rest of the family. They were looking for a larger house with a basement in a nicer part of town. Their son Chris was a teenager. They suggested that the two families go together and buy a better house than either of us could afford alone. We looked at many houses and finally chose one with a half basement that made a good place for Leonard and me. It had high windows for light and enjoyment of the scenery and two entrances which we thought quite important. The house was convenient, well-built and situated in a very nice neighborhood; we enjoyed living there.

CHAPTER SEVENTEEN

WICHITA THE SECOND TIME

Joy and Denny went to an Evangelical Free Church, so we went there too. After a short time, we felt it was just too big to suit us, so we transferred to a smaller E. Free Church a little closer to home. There we learned that a new E. Free Church was forming in Derby, a small town about ten miles away. The church was meeting in the new, large high school building. Leonard and I decided we would like to be in on the starting of a new group, so for several years we drove there each Sunday. It was a good experience.

Joy had taken the position of children's director at her church. At that time it was a part-time job. After a time it was evident that the position really required a full-time director. Joy still had a son in high school, her parents to supervise, and several other interests, so she did not want a full-time position. The E. Free churches, however, had begun a city mission in a poor part of town where a lot of Hispanic people lived, so Joy volunteered to be children's minister there. Actually, Denny had helped start this group, teaching Bible classes Sunday afternoons. The group looked for a full-time pastor and asked Denny, but he felt he could not take the position at that time. The group searched and found a pastor, and the funny thing about it was that his name was also Dennis. And if that weren't enough, guess what! His wife's name, of course, was Joy! The two Joy's and two Dennis' became very good friends.

Leonard and I helped at this mission in a number of ways. We helped with tutoring and special events, and I found other ways to be useful there. I made banners to make the gym where the group met look more like church. I also crafted a number of items and taught some of the older children to sew or embroider. At one point I made complete outfits for dolls. I found used dolls in the secondhand store and cleaned, repaired and dressed them, and they then looked quite beautiful. We sold them at the mission craft sales and gained some money for the church.

A local senior center was located not far from home. We began going there for exercise. One class offered chair exercises. Older people can lose their balance when standing and then fall, so these chair exercises were safer but can be of as much benefit. We went two times weekly for years and I'm sure it helped us a lot. I was invited to teach a Bible class there and did for years. Also, through these classes, word got to a local nursing home where I also taught several years. So we had plenty of good activities and were happy, comfortable and busy enough.

This went on for several years. Leonard was limited because of his failing eyesight, but he enjoyed gardening and produced plenty of fresh vegetables. He also did much yard work and in the house he did most of the vacuuming. Sometimes I would remind him, "Honey, it's the day to vacuum the front room." And he would say, "No, it isn't; I just did that yesterday." He was losing track of time. In many ways we began to see that his mind was not working properly. We were convinced that he was showing signs of Alzheimer's disease. His strength was failing some and his mental condition was worsening.

Finally, we decided that a nursing home could give him better care than we could. We found a good facility quite close to home so I was able to visit him often, almost every day. It was not luxurious but sufficient and provided good care. The patients were carefully monitored. There were group activities to keep them functioning together. This section was locked so the patients would not wander off and get lost. Once they were not going to let me out, as they thought I was one of the patients.

One morning they called to say that Leonard had fallen and cut a small gash in his forehead. They were sending him to the hospital. The wound was cared for and he was returned to the nursing home. A couple of days later, it was discovered that he had also broken a hip in his fall, so he was sent back to the hospital. The hip was repaired. I was at the hospital much of the time while he was there. In a few days he was permitted to return to the nursing home. He received special care and the break and wound seemed to heal normally, but he was never the same. He just did not regain his strength.

About a month later, the nurses put him in a special room reserved for those who were dying. I cared for him just as I had for others when working as a nurse. In just a few hours, he left us. We had made arrangements for the body to be given to the Kansas University School of Medicine. A comforting memorial service was held at the church where Joy was working and we both had served. The pastor of that church and the pastor of my Friends church were present to comfort. Friends provided beautiful music.

That was about seven years ago. I have learned what it is to be a widow. One simply goes on, though there is such a lonely, empty space. I enjoy crafts and usually have something in progress to occupy my hands and mind. Now I am writing this book.

I enjoy my good home with daughter Joy and her husband Denny. I am so thankful to them and to the Lord that I have a nice home, all my needs cared for. I thank God for His help and comfort. I rejoice in the good life Leonard and I had during the sixty-six years we were together. Most importantly, I rejoice in the blessed hope we have. Death in this world is not the end. We expect to meet again in the beautiful home prepared for us. We will rejoice in the presence of our Heavenly Father and our Lord Jesus.

I thank the Lord for caring for me all these years and for saving my soul so that I can look forward to a glorious future. I thank Him now for good health and an enjoyable life. I can walk, though a bit wobbly at times, go up and down stairs many times each day, walk around the block, enjoy water aerobics each week, and chew with my own teeth.

True, I have trouble hearing so I wear two hearing aids. My left eye has succumbed to macular degeneration. Periodically, I get injections in the right eye to save my sight in that eye and it is doing fairly well. I clean our kitchen and my rooms each week and attend one or two cultural activities with my daughter. I help with the Sunday School lesson. As you see, I am busy and seldom bored. I thank the Lord for my many friends, for health and strength and all His blessings.

LEONARD IN NURSING HOME WITH LEIGH

FOUR GRANDCHILDREN

DAUGHTER JOY & HUSBAND,
LEIGH & LEONARD

60TH WEDDING ANNIVERSARY

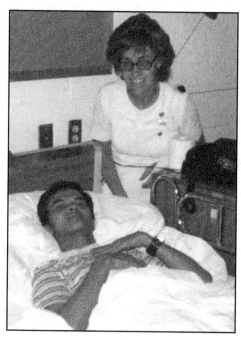

LEIGH AT WORK - NURSING

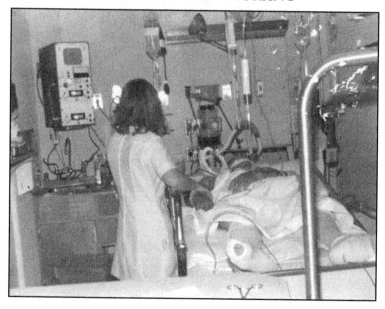

LEONARD PREACHING

LEONARD WITH SASIMON ON HIS VISIT TO U.S.

CHAPTER EIGHTEEN
ADDENDA

ADAPTATIONS

Living in the rainforest would be quite different from life in the USA. Our location was just about the middle of Africa, east, west and north, south. We were a long way from either coast; hence, transportation was both difficult and expensive. We made use of the resources of the jungle when possible. We did import such things as cook stoves, saw mill, brick press, metal bedsteads, gasoline, cement, and other necessities.

Most of our houses were made native style. Eventually, we did construct two brick houses, two cement block ones and a native rock one. Balega style was mud walls supported by pokes, branches and vines, then plastered with mud and whitewashed. Mud made good insulation against the heat. Roofs were leaves tied onto rafters with vines.

A veranda was made all around as protection for the mud walls from rain. Our mission had a rich deposit of slate which were thin slabs of rocks. These made good floors, often a problem in Africa. A few nails, hinges, wire, and glass were all that was needed except some local supplies. A missionary house needed four outside doors: one each for the front room, kitchen, office and bath. Closets needed a window to help keep things dry.

Some of our furniture was made of local valuable woods such as mahogany. We used wooden packing boxes as cupboards. Some wicker chairs and couches were available. Pillows and even small mattresses could be made of Congo cotton materials and stuffed with cotton or kapok or chicken or duck feathers if available. The Africans usually stuffed their pillows with dried leaves or grass. At night we used mosquito nets around our beds to protect from mosquitoes and other insects. Netting could be bought at the store and also cheap muslin to reinforce edges and tops. With these resources one could make a quite comfortable home.

People often ask, "But what did you have as food?" As with houses, we used the local foods when available. Local products in our area were manioc, rice, greens, hot peppers, peanuts, and many kinds of tropical fruit such as bananas, papayas, mangoes, pineapples, avocados, lemons, passion fruit and grapefruit. For staples we could order things in case lots from our city stores about 150 miles away. These included canned or powdered milk, tomato paste, oatmeal, butter, cheese, and corned beef from Argentina. We considered the best cook the one who could fix corned beef in the most original ways.

Food preparation was more difficult there. First, we had to start a fire in the cook stove with wood from the forest; of course, this worked better if the wood was dried. The Balega cooked over an open fire. Cooking and drinking water came from a spring at the bottom of the hill. We boiled and filtered the water before drinking. If we wanted peanut butter, we roasted, shelled and ground the peanuts. We roasted and ground coffee also. We had no electric mixers, grinders, bread makers, can openers, or fans. We used what was at hand.

Local people often brought produce to our door for us to buy. Sometimes it might be a chicken or fish or eggs. If we did not get enough eggs, we would send a boy out to the villages to buy some. He took with him some money and a pail of water to test the eggs. If one floated, it was a bad egg. For refrigeration, we had a contraption of two large balls connected with a large pipe. Each morning the large ball was slowly heated over an open fire. When just right, it was brought into the pantry and placed in a pail of water; the smaller ball rested inside a large insulated box. The chemical in the balls would heat, evaporate, cool and condense, thus producing cold like a refrigerator. It was not really good but better than open air. Later, we acquired regular Serbel refrigerators from Sweden which were operated with kerosene.

One of the favorite Balega foods was rice served with greens and hot pepper sauce, and I do mean HOT. The Balega raised rice on the hillsides. After harvesting, they pounded it to remove the husks. It was good white rice. They also used manioc for carbohydrates. They dried one kind of manioc and pounded it into fine flour about like cornstarch. This they then made into a damp bread. We liked manioc coarsely ground and then baked as a casserole, maybe with a little cheese on top. It was important not to mix or stir it; if you did, it would become very gummy. One kind of manioc was poisonous until it had been soaked for a time. The Balega would make a little side place in a stream and put the harvested manioc there. It made quite a bad smell at first. This they dried and then pounded to make fine flour. As they dried it over an open fire, it always tasted smoky to us.

Keeping clean clothes was sometimes a problem. Our laundry worker washed the clothes in a simple type of hand-operated washing machine with a hand-operated wringer. We made a clothesline, but the climate was so damp that sometimes it took two days to dry the clothes. Then he used a charcoal iron to press clothes.

For personal cleanliness, we had a wash bowl and pitcher of water in the bathroom. For baths, we made a tub of half a gasoline barrel cut lengthwise. We attached supports to keep it from rolling. Bath water could be heated in the cook stove's reservoir. We had a drain in the middle of the floor so dirty water could just be poured down the drain. A cesspool had been dug out in the backyard and covered with a network of branches and vines, covered with earth and grass like the rest of the lawn. A channel had been dug from the bathroom through the veranda to the underground pool. Cold water from the rain barrel did for hands.

The toilet was flushed by getting a pail of water from the rain barrel on the veranda. I helped make our toilet. First, I formed a drainpipe of mud with curves for a water trap, then let it dry well. The carpenters made a wooden form and poured cement into the form, carefully positioning my mud pipe. When the cement had fully dried, the mud was washed out of the channel. Carpenters produced a wooden seat and voila! Later, we rigged up a shower. We put a large water barrel in the attic; water was heated in the cook stove's reservoir and carried upstairs by our helpers. A space in the bath was curtained off and a drain made in the floor. All the convenience of home in the USA! There was another cesspool for the kitchen wastes. It is really amazing what can be accomplished when the need arises.

THE BABY'S BED

Our fourth child, Ruth Gay, was almost two when we arrived at Ikozi the second time. When we reached Ikozi, we were given the use of a fairly new brick house, very nice except that there was only one bedroom for the six of us. We remodeled and made the dining room into our room. The attic was finished so we put beds for Joy and Len up there, but we could not find a suitable, safe bed for toddler Gay. We had shipped out a large case of toilet paper (not readily available in Congo). This case was longer than Gay was. I took out all the paper rolls and then replaced them sidewise; thus, the rolls were a little squishy, more like a mattress. With pad, blanket and sheet, this made a comfortable bed for her, temporary, of course. She soon grew too tall to fit.

This reminds me of other unusual beds our children had to use for a time. Joy and Happy (Len) had a long narrow cot. They could sleep one at each end, with their feet almost together. Then baby Merry Sue, when an infant, had an empty dresser drawer for a crib. We once made a bed for Melodie when she was about five on a wide closet shelf. When Merry Sue was about eight months old, we were on a trip and needed a

237

bed for her. Leonard found a canvas army cot and cut it down shorter. Then I devised a system of belts to fit around the cot and then to the baby. She could turn from side to side but not fall out. At one time or another, each of our children had a strange bed. We were thankful that was only temporary, in some cases only for a night or two.

LUGGAGE

When we were ready to come home for our third furlough, we needed another piece of luggage. Where would one find a new suitcase in the jungle? Before this time, friends in the USA had given us a set of Tupperware containers. One was a large box about sixteen inches square. I made a cover of some sturdy Congolese cloth just to fit; I used zippers to close it and straps as handles. It made quite a handy case of lightweight luggage that served us all the way home. I still use it today; it is so handy. It has since had three new covers.

LAUNDRY

Not all adaptations have to occur in foreign lands. During our first furlough, we had to travel much. We then had two older children and a baby. This was before convenient motels and handy laundry facilities. Keeping clean clothes was a problem. We devised our own washing machine. We found a metal cream can with a tight-fitting lid. In the morning I would put warm water and soap powder in the can and then add the dirty clothes. The can then went in the car trunk, and the motion of the car swished the clothes about and cleaned them. When we stopped for the night, I rinsed the clothes and strung them about our room, hoping they would dry. Sometimes we held those damp clothes out the back right car window to finish drying them as we traveled along. We were thankful that we could manage that much in our travels.

MORE STORIES

BUTCHER SHOPS

While we were living in Brussels, we found there were many butcher shops, each carrying only one type of meat. There were shops for beef, others for pork, still others for horse meat. We learned to like horse meat quite well, though most Americans avoided it. Later, while working in the Belgian Congo, a new missionary family arrived. They also had had a stay in Belgium. One day a fellow missionary was planning a trip to the city for supplies. As usual, he asked if anyone would like for him to bring something back. These people said, "Oh, yes, please bring us some of that good dried beef." Well, there wasn't any dried beef so he brought them dried horse meat. They ate and enjoyed it. No one ever told them it was horse meat.

SPECIAL DELIVERY

For a time we had delivery services. A truck would pick up supplies and orders in our city, Bakavu, and bring them out to the jungle, once a week. The truck was loaded just as the supplies arrived at the warehouse with no concern for their destination. Then it took a full day to reach our station. The driver picked up items and people all along the way.

A mile beyond us was a large river that had to be crossed by native ferry. Often the truck would not stop at our station because it was too much work to unload everything to find our order. So the truck would proceed on to the end of the route, about fifty miles beyond. There they unloaded everything and left what had been ordered for that place. Then the truck would come all the way back to unload our things. Can you imagine what "fresh" vegetables looked like after a week on the road? The crates and baskets probably had been sat on by a mother with a small child. We learned to listen for that truck. If it did not stop at our driveway, our men would rush up the road where the truck had to wait to board the ferry. There they would insist that our things be unloaded. Of course, if the supplies had been loaded efficiently, it would not have been difficult to unload our things as the truck passed. I doubt that they ever learned.

COINCIDENCES

AFRICA

While we were out of the Congo, we worked awhile in Rwanda and Burundi. Our two middle girls were able to attend a school for missionary children named Mweya. It was maintained by the Free Methodists, Friends and a third mission group. There were about sixteen children in school and most of them were living in the school dormitory. Katherine Hendricks was the teacher of all the grades. The dorm parents were the Millers who had two boys and one little girl, Ruthie. Our girls were there portions of two school years while we worked at a Free Methodist station just about a half hour away.

243

Our girls and Ruthie Miller were grown up and married when we retired and moved to Ozark, Arkansas, to help in a Christian school. There was a Free Methodist church in the little town, but it was closed for lack of a pastor. Before long, however, a new pastor, Rev. Vance, came to repair and reopen that church. News gets around in a small town and many people knew that we had been missionaries in Africa. The new pastor and his wife were interested to learn more about us. Who was this pastor's wife? Katherine Hendricks, now Vance, who had taught Sue and Gay in Mweya, Africa.

Many years later, we moved to Wichita, Kansas, and started attending a Friends church near our home. Before long we learned that the daughter of a Friends missionary couple from Burundi attended there. Who do you suppose this was? Ruthie Miller! She is now a grandmother and her name is Ruth Kemper. One Sunday her parents, the Millers, attended our church from a nearby town. So here are two coincidences arising from the same situation, namely the Millers being the dorm parents of our children in Burundi!

FURNITURE

Our oldest daughter Joy lived awhile in Baltimore, Maryland. While there, she attended an estate sale and bought a charming roll-top desk.

It was rather small and had probably been built for a child. We all liked it very much, but it had drawbacks. The space between the drawers below was quite narrow and the desk was sold without a chair. For months we looked for a chair narrow enough to fit the space. Months later I visited an antique furniture store in Wichita. I was about to leave when I noticed a small swivel desk chair. As I checked out the chair, there on the bottom was stamped its place of origin, New Paris, Maine. Sometime later I visited my daughter, now living in Dallas, and took this chair; she was very pleased. One day we were cleaning her house. I moved out the desk to sweep behind it and found a name stamped on the back of the desk, New Paris, Maine. Apparently, the desk, manufactured in Maine, had been bought and sold in Baltimore, moved to Dallas, and its matching chair was found in Wichita, Kansas.

NAMES

Leonard and I were engaged just as I started nurse's training. Several other girls had serious boyfriends. One of them had a friend named John Parsons. The name "Parson" is a word associated with churches and pastors. So here we have Leonard Parcel who became an ordained Christian missionary pastor, and John Parson who ended up working at the Post Office. One might think their last names were mixed up.

I taught a Bible class at a nursing home in Wichita where I gave my name as Leigh. A few weeks later I confided to a special friend at the nursing home that Leigh was not my first name, but the one I preferred. She replied by asking, "What is your first name, then?" I replied, "Hazel." And what do you think she said then? "That's my first name, too." I knew her as Maurine but her full name was Hazel Maurine. We had fun calling each other Hazel!

Our daughter Joy married Dennis Domen. Dennis was instrumental in starting a small urban church. At first, it was only a Sunday afternoon Bible class, but it grew into a church and needed a full-time pastor. Dennis could not become the pastor because of his secular work in a facility for delinquent youth. The church finally found a pastor whose name was Dennis and his wife's name was Joy! Thus, the church had two couples named Dennis and Joy. We called our Dennis, Denny, and the pastor, Dennis. People still had to specify which Joy they wanted.

FRIENDS

I liked to fellowship a moment between Sunday School and church with a man at the Friends church in Wichita. We had some interesting encounters. One day I was walking toward an outer door and at that moment he entered from outside. Another time I entered a large room from the west and just that moment he entered from the east. It happened several times that he would be walking along a hall and just as he passed, I would come out of a room opening into that hall, and vice versa. Did all these just happen, or did God really intend us to become friends? Also, there were some other unusual facts. He had a daughter whose middle name was Joy, the middle name of our daughter Joy. His daughter-in-law was Melody; our youngest is Melodie. His daughter had a friend Anthony and our grandson is Anthony. He had a granddaughter named Lacey and I have a niece Lacey.

When my mother was a little girl, her father, a carpenter, was working in Southwest Oklahoma in Indian Territory near a little town called Gotebo. It was named for the Indian chief of the area. He was quite cooperative with the white people. There was a stream nearby that often flooded. Once my mother was swept downstream by a flood. The chief Gotebo came out in his canoe and rescued her. This story has been passed down in our family for years.

Recently, I met a couple in our Sunday School class. He is quite a writer and writes a column in a small town newspaper about the early days. I asked one day if I could see one of his writings. He gave me a copy and what do you suppose? It was about a little town named Gotebo.

When next I saw him, I asked, "What do you know about Gotebo?" Was he surprised to learn that I also knew about this same small town?

MISSIONS

Many years ago I was studying world missions. I decided that it would be profitable to select one country, learning more about it and praying for its people. For no apparent reason I chose Nepal. I learned there were very few Christians in the whole country. One of the few was a man named Prem Padhan. He was put in prison because of his faith in Jesus so I prayed for him and his country. He was content to be in prison for he could teach the other prisoners about Jesus. Many of these were political prisoners and could wield great influence if they ever got out. If they knew God, it could be a help to the whole country. Finally Prem was released.

Many years later a couple came to our church to tell about their work. They were going to Nepal to work in a hospital. Their family name was Padan. This I thought was a great coincidence. We sent to their support for years and were able to visit them when they were on furlough.

Still more years later I attended a very good Friends church. It was only two blocks from our home. In this church two families of missionaries from Nepal told about the work there. A few of our church people had even gone to Nepal for short-term missionary service. They returned and told us about the progress there. How does it happen that my church is so interested in Nepal? Surely God wanted me to be involved, in some small way, with missions in Nepal. At the beginning of my interest, there were very few Christians. Today there are at least forty churches of converted Hindus who love Jesus.

AUTOMOBILE

In 1989 Leonard and I bought a new Chevy Geo Prism. It was a very good car and we used it over twenty years. In or about 2011, I was told that the transmission was about to go out, but it would be all right to drive it very carefully a while longer. I really wanted to be able to say I had driven when I was ninety-seven. Birthday ninety-seven came and went and I was still driving. But the second day I was ninety-seven it happened! I had wondered where I would be when it occurred. Would it be a long way from home? How would I get help? We live three blocks from our church. I was in the church parking lot when my car quit working. Someone at the church took me safely home. The Lord not only granted my desire but guarded my safety as well.

CONCLUSION

Now as I have passed my 101st birthday, I look back over my life with a sense of thankfulness and satisfaction. Though there have been trials, difficulties, dangers, and tragedies, in the main it has been a happy life. I thank the Lord for making it worthwhile. I have never regretted any of my major decisions. First, I accepted Jesus as my personal Savior at the age of seventeen. He has been my protector and guide ever since. Second, I chose to attend a four-year Bible college, followed by a four-year nursing school.

At Bible school I met my future husband, Leonard. We were married and raised five dear children. After school we chose to go to Africa as missionaries. Yes, if it were possible, I would do it all over again.

However, I would hope to avoid my mistakes, sins, and failures along the way.

The Lord has given me the desires of my heart: a satisfying career, a happy marriage, a family, and many wonderful experiences.

Though it might have seemed a sacrifice to go to Africa, it made possible many amazing adventures. I have seen oceans, lakes, rivers, fertile fields, mountains, canyons, deserts, and forests; the land of Israel, the Swiss Alps, principal cities as New York City, London, Brussels, Lisbon, Cairo, and Jerusalem. I have seen some famous people: Helen Keller, Charles Lindbergh, Billy Sunday, and the King of Burundi. Many of these would not have come my way if I had not gone to Africa. All my children had the advantage of living for a time in another culture and with another language, receiving a good basic education in our mission schools, traveling to several different countries, meeting many interesting people, and making many friends. It has enriched their lives. Sometimes as I recall certain situations, I marvel and say, "However did I manage that?" I am sure it was because God helped me greatly.

Yes, I must admit that it has been an amazing life. Now as I approach the end of this earthly journey, I know that the best is yet to come. I am looking forward to life in God's beautiful heaven. I am assured that I will be admitted there because Jesus is the one and only way and I trust Him. He made the way for me and for you and for the whole world. He took the punishment for our sins and paid our debt when He died upon the cruel Cross. What a joy it will be to arrive in heaven and see Jesus! One hundred years here and then glorious life with Him! I gave Him a little and He has returned it a hundred fold. My heart can only say, "Oh, the wonder of it all!"

ADVICE FOR LONGEVITY

Since I have passed the 100-year mark, I am often asked the secret of long life. I believe that God has a plan for each life, including life span. "He numbers our days." "Our times are in His hands."

Another factor is one's heredity. "It's in the genes." God gives us each a soul and a body. The build and strength of that body has been handed down through the generations. Some are made stronger than others. We just have to accept what has come to us. However, each one can modify that plan by his lifestyle. I divided these influences into three categories: Attitude, Ailments (Diet), and Activity.

ATTITUDE. We consider such attitudes as anxiety, worry, and stress as concerns of the emotions, but they can greatly affect physical health as well. Develop a peaceful, happy outlook on life. "Commit your way unto the Lord and He will direct your paths." He can calm the worries and give you a calm, confident attitude. He has promised to carry our burdens if we love Him and let Him.

AILMENTS, DIET. What we put into our bodies is very important. God gave food to Adam and Eve. They could eat the fruit of many fruit trees, except one. He also gave them the "herbs of the field" which could include vegetables and grains. Modern dieticians tell us that we need a balanced diet with carbohydrates, proteins and fats. Adam was not to eat animal meat, but there was plenty of protein in several grains and vegetables as soy, peas, and many kinds of beans. We should eat a large proportion of carbohydrates, a smaller amount of protein and a still smaller proportion of oils or fats. There are a number of vegetable fats, including corn, nuts, and also olives. Vegetarians can still enjoy a balanced diet.

As important as what we do, eat or drink is what we should not put into our bodies. Alcoholic drinks, tobacco, and drugs are very harmful and do promote early death. It is also wise to limit the amount of salt, sugar, fats, and carbonated drinks. "Taste and see that the Lord is good." "He gives us richly all things to enjoy." We may think that overindulgence gives pleasure, but it is only momentary and leads to terrible consequences. "Eat what is good."

ACTIVITY. As people grow older, they have a tendency to seek comfort and rest. This is just what makes them old. While you are alive, LIVE! KEEP ACTIVE! Enjoy a hobby, join a group, attend church and Sunday School, attend some cultural and entertaining events. Take regular exercise or walks. Be friendly and make many friends. You may think you don't have the time or strength to do these things, but doing at least one of them will give you an interest in life, make life worthwhile, and keep you young. Of course with activity comes the necessity for rest. Many older people find that they need more sleep than when they were younger. A good sleep at night is important. In the daytime it is good to alternate periods of exercise with rest periods, times of work with times for recreation.

If you want a long, happy life, remember these: ATTITUDE, AILMENTS, and ACTIVITY.

When we were planning to go to Africa, people warned us that we would be taking our children into great danger, danger from wild animals, insects, and disease germs. However, with a few precautions, we found life in the jungle to be quite beneficial. Here are some of the advantages:

We had clean air. The forest is full of green trees. The green color is caused by a substance called chlorophyll. This enables the trees to take in carbon dioxide (our waste) and exude oxygen (their waste). Thus, we had an oxygen-rich atmosphere. Beside, the almost daily rains washed the air and kept it fresh. We had no fumes or smog. An automobile might pass our station once every two or three days.

We had clean water with no industrial poisons or such. True, it might carry disease germs, but we avoided that by boiling and filtering the water which we used for drinking and cooking. We used rainwater for baths, cleaning, etc. We had a system of rain troughs and large barrels to keep rainwater. Our drinking water came from a spring at the bottom of our hill.

A large part of our food was raised locally on garden plots cleared out of the jungle. Fertilizers were the natural forest debris with no chemical additives. The gardens had lots of sunshine, moisture, fresh air, and natural fertilizers. So we had organic food. Some vegetables might carry germs which we avoided by soaking in a permanganate solution. All together, we fared very well and avoided some of the evils of civilized life.

Now I have arrived at the venerable age of 101. I am quite healthy, active and happy.

MY YEARS IN ZAIRE

ere is the story from the husband's viewpoint. In three pages he tells what took his wife seventeen chapters to tell. Zaire was the name Congo took just after independence. Now, however, it is known as the Democratic Republic of Congo (DRC).

In August 1944, I left Philadelphia on a Portuguese liner bound for Lisbon. It was an exciting day, actually being on my way to Africa after many delays, but also a sad day. I was leaving behind my wife and two children, not knowing it would be a long twenty-seven months before they could join me in Zaire.

There was a long delay in Portugal and I did not arrive on the field until December. There were at that time only five missionaries of Berean Mission, all working at Ikozi station. Katanti station had been opened by Albert and Mamie Jansen during their first term. When they returned after furlough, the Jansens and Parcels were assigned to Katanti. After a bit, two other women joined us there.

My first task was to study the tribal language, Kilega. After I had gained a speaking knowledge of Kilega, the rest of the term was occupied with some preaching of the Word and a great deal of teaching in the primary school for the Balega children. While Bible lessons were a prominent part, we also taught math, history and other classes that the Balega teachers were not qualified to teach. Sundays we sometimes went to other villages for services with people who did not often get to come to the station church. These trips were limited because we did not have a car.

We were granted our first furlough in 1950. We were taking three children home with us. Merry Sue was only three months old; her bed on the plane was a pillow. After furlough, we started back in 1952 with four children, Gay having been born in Denver. Our first stop was in Belgium where I studied French and Hazel Leigh completed a course in tropical medicine. This gave her recognition as a Sanitary Agent with authority to operate a rural dispensary.

Again, we were first stationed at Ikozi, but were soon transferred to Katanti. There a three-year Bible school had been started for the Balega, and a school for missionary children was opened. There was also an elementary school through fifth grade for the Balega children. Hazel Leigh was kept busy with the dispensary. Much of my time was occupied in overseeing the construction of much needed buildings. Then it was furlough time for one of the Bible school teachers, so I had to find time to teach in the Bible school also.

This time we had our own vehicle, a pickup with a homemade cover. We went often to villages on Sundays and several times took extended trips, taking Balega evangelists with me to do the preaching and Hazel Leigh to pass out medicines and help with children's meetings.

During this term, Berean Mission opened its fifth station, this one among the Bakumu people. They did not speak Kilega, so Swahili, a tribal language, was used there.

Even during our best days in Zaire, to visit all five of our stations required at least two full days. It was 225 miles from one extreme to the other over very crooked, mountainous roads, often muddy and sometimes beset with landslides.

Again, our family membership changed, and upon our second furlough we brought home five children, the latest, Melodie, born in 1956. Then in 1959 we returned to Zaire with only four. Joy, our oldest, stayed with friends (the Ernest Lott family) to complete high school and go on to Bible schooling and nurse's training.

Zaire gained independence in 1960. That brought changes in missionary work. War broke out and the fighting was not far from our area. Our Balega leaders advised the missionaries to go across the border for a time. After about six weeks, we were able to return. Meanwhile, some missionaries went to other places, shuffling the remaining workers. The Parcels and Carl Moyer were assigned to the Bakumu station, Uku. Sadly, our stay there was short, about four months. Civil war was not yet over.

A conference was called to discuss our situation and determine action. While it was in session, we were visited by the Simba (rebel soldiers). Conditions were very tense for a few minutes, but the Simbas left after they were convinced that we had no firearms. They confiscated our radio transmitter-receivers, leaving us with no means of communication.

The African elders convinced us that it would be better for both us and them if we vacated the area. We took their advice but had quite some difficulty crossing the border. This time we were out eighteen months, during which time the Parcels helped out at Free Methodist stations in Ruanda and Burundi.

Upon return, we found considerable damage had been done to books and possessions but buildings were intact. The few of us still there were all at our most central station, Katchingu, for a time. Then the Parcels went to reopen Katanti. A few students were still at the Bible school, so

I helped with the teaching there while Hazel Leigh served at the dispensary and taught Melodie.

Many evenings we visited villages both directions from home, giving simple teaching in Bible doctrine to village Christians. We had not heard of the TEE program, but that is about what we tried to do, gearing it to the simple village people.

Our third furlough came in 1964. We were happy that we could be home just in time for Joy's graduation from nursing school. On the way we were able to visit Israel, Cairo, Switzerland, and the World's Fair in New York.

Before leaving our field, we had heard that arms were being smuggled into Zaire again, so we were not very surprised that war soon broke out again. Considerable time elapsed before peace came to that troubled country.

We are glad that the church continues to grow, that the Bible school is operating, that leaders are being trained to guide the church and teach in the many schools in the area, and that some of the medical workers have become very well trained.

We praise God for letting us have a part in those early years of Berean Mission in Zaire.

JUNGLE SONG

The jungle is a'bumble

The jungle is a'grumble

The birds and beasts

Are busy as can be;

But in this jungly bumble

And in the bumbly jungle

There is magic for me.

The jungle is a'mumble

The jungle is a'tumble

The flow'rs and trees

And vines grow ceaselessly;

But in this jungly tumble

And in this tumbly jungle

There is beauty for me.

The jungle is a'jumble
The jungle is a'tumble
The rain and winds
And streams are winding through;
But in this jungly tumble
And in this tumbly jungle
There'll be beauty for you.

The jungle is a'grumble
The jungle is a'rumble
The native drums
Are pounding rhythmic'ly;
But in this grumbly rumble
And in this rumbly jungle
There's a challenge for me.

Oh, come and see the jungle
Tell the heathen as they fumble
Of God's great love
And life in Christ anew;
Then in this jungly jumble
And in this jumbly jungle
There'll be real joy for you.

AFTERWORD

W ell, this is months later after I finished the main part. Much has happened since then and the book was laid aside.

Joy's husband Denny died, and Joy and I sold our house and now live in a nice, smaller apartment in a very convenient location. About six weeks after our move, I fell and broke my pelvic bone. After six weeks at a rehabilitation facility, I was able to return home.

I resumed working on my book and hope it will soon be ready for publishing. Meanwhile, I celebrated my 101st birthday.

CPSIA information can be obtained at www.ICGtesting.com
Printed in the USA
LVOW04s2319061114

412191LV00003B/4/P